The Marketing Cookbook for Translators

Foolproof recipes for a thriving freelance translation career

By **Tess Whitty**

Translator and host of the Marketing Tips for Translators podcast

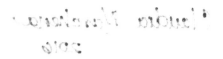

Translation Services is responsible for the success or failure of your business decisions.

Although the author and publisher have made every effort to ensure that the information in this book was correct at press time, the author and publisher do not assume and hereby disclaim any liability to any party for any loss, damage, or disruption caused by errors or omissions, whether such errors or omissions result from negligence, accident, or any other cause.

Table of Contents

Legal Disclaimer 2

About the Author 8

Acknowledgements 11

Introduction 12

    How to use this book 14

Chapter 1 Your Pantry..17

    1.1: The Lay of the Land..19

    1.2: Twelve Common Mistakes..28

    1.3: Choosing Specializations...40

    1.4: Buying Training Ingredients 48

    1.5: Tools for a successful translation career 52

Chapter 2 Appetizers 59

    Recipe 1: *Your Business Foundation* 60

    Recipe 2: *SMART Goals* 66

    Steps 67

    Recipe 3: *SWOT Analysis*..74

    Recipe 4: *The Marketing plan* 80

Chapter 3 94

Your Basic Marketing Tools 94

    Recipe 5: *Resume*..97

Recipe 6: *Cover Letter* 103

Recipe 7: *Business Cards* 113

Chapter 4 116

Magnetic Marketing Tools 116

Recipe 8: *Your website* 117

Chapter 5: Magnetic Marketing Tools: Social Media, Referrals, Testimonials and Publicity 131

Recipe 9: *LinkedIn* 136

Recipe 10: *Twitter* 150

Recipe 11: *Facebook* 162

Recipe 12: *Google+* 171

Recipe 13: *Blogging* 175

Recipe 14: *Networking* 185

Recipe 15: *Referrals and testimonials* 191

Referrals 194

Recipe 16: *Publicity* 198

Little book of PR for translators, by Nicole Y. Adams. Master the Art of Public Speaking: How to Give a Great Speech with Confidence and Actually Enjoy Speaking in Public, by K. C. McAllister. 207

Recipe 17: *Advertising* 211

Chapter 6 Entrées 214

Where to find clients 214

Recipe 18: *Translation Portals and Directories* 217

Recipe 19: *Translation Agencies* 220

Recipe 20: *Direct Clients* 227

Chapter 7 Side Dishes 238

Recipe 21: *Pricing strategies for your translation services* ..239

Recipe 22: *Pricing Structure* 244

Recipe 23: *Raising your rates* 251

Chapter 8 Desserts..255

Recipe 24: *Customer Care* 256

Recipe 25: *Feast and Famine Strategies* 261

Balance 266

Chapter 9 Conclusion 277

Appendix...278

About the Author
Tess Whitty

My name is Tess Whitty, and I have been an English-to-Swedish translator since 2003. During the past decade I have practiced and learned most of what you will need to know in order to market your translation services and build a thriving translation business. While I was completing my Master's degrees in International Marketing and Business Communications and PR, I had no idea that I was going to become a translator, even though I loved studying languages (at one point I knew six languages). Instead I focused on international marketing and started working as a marketing assistant in 2006, working my way up to a product marketing manager position for a telecommunications and IT company in Sweden. It was not until I moved to the US with my husband, plus a toddler, and another baby on the way, that I started looking into other ways of making a living so that I could balance making a living and taking care of my family.

One day one of my friends said, "Why don't you start working as a translator? You are completely fluent in two languages, are good at writing and grammar, and have strong business skills." So, I strongly considered her suggestion. I did some research and decided to give it a try. After my first job as a freelance translator I have never looked back, and it has been one of my life's most fulfilling endeavors.

There are quite a few business books for freelance translators out there. I have read most of them and consider them very valuable and recommend them to my colleagues. My reason for writing yet another one is this — I wanted to focus on practical marketing techniques that translators could use to grow their client bases and take their businesses to the next level.

Given my professional background and education in international marketing, I decided to start sharing some of my knowledge by presenting at conferences, giving webinars and blogging about different marketing topics for translators. This book, *The Marketing Cookbook for Translators*, is a culmination of those efforts. It contains over a decade's worth of experience learned firsthand as I constructed my own thriving business in the growing translation industry. My hope is that you are able to benefit from this knowledge and apply these simple marketing recipes to your own life and business. I wish you every success and I look forward to you taking this journey with me.

Acknowledgements

This book is dedicated to my family — You are the inspiration behind everything I do and the reason I started my freelance translation business. Thank you!

Editing: Madeline Blasberg
Proofreading: Kammy Wood.

A special thanks to the following colleagues who have contributed to this book:

Nicole Y. Adams, Ryan Becker, Anne Diamantidis, Ed Gandia, Johanna Gonzalés, Sebastian Haselbeck, Judy and Dagmar Jenner, Gwenydd Jones, Alessandra Martelli, Corinne McKay, Joy Mo, Beth Podrovitz, A.M. Sall, Jill Sommer, Luke Spear, Laura Spencer, Julieta Spirito, Jiri Stejskal Marta Stelmaszak, Louisa Stockley, Carol Tice, Susan Ward, Levent Yildizgoren, and Maja Źróbecka.

Thank you also to all linguists and colleagues who have shown support for my idea for this book, for the Marketing Tips for Translators podcast, and for helping me pick a title and cover for this book. You are my motivation!

Tess Whitty

November 2014

Introduction

Translators are meticulous people. But making the leap between earning a certification or getting your degree and building a thriving translation business can be daunting. Navigating the sea of competition, establishing a consistent brand, attracting and retaining clients – it can be a lot to tackle. But it can also be a fulfilling business that provides you with a steady stream of income and the freedom to be your own boss.

Over the past decade I have built my own translation company from the ground up, making mistakes along the way and learning from every experience. Over time I came to learn that business building draws upon many of the same skills required of a translator. There's a big picture, but there's also a formula – steps to follow that are designed to take the guesswork out of the game.

I have met many translators who struggle to find their footing in the business world, many of them feeling underqualified and poorly prepared. Translation degrees usually do not provide enough marketing skills and if you are transferring to a translation career from another field, you might also need some marketing training to get your business to really thrive.

If you find yourself feeling at a loss for how to structure your business, set your prices, attract and retain clients – then I want you to know that I have been there. I have navigated through the same challenges that you are facing right now, and I have enjoyed a successful career.

Don't you wish that marketing your translation services were as easy as following a recipe in a cookbook? I know I do. I am by no means a great chef, but I can produce pretty decent food by following proven recipes in a cookbook.

In my experience, the recipes and principles contained in this book have produced positive results for translators at every stage in the game and should for you, as well, whether you are a translator who is:

- Interested in creating a freelance business or have recently launched a business

- In need of proven marketing tactics and step-by-step strategies to create a steady stream of income

- Wanting to take your translation career to the next level, or polish your marketing tactics

If you find yourself in one of the above categories, hungry for the skills and strategies that will take your business to the next level – then I'm glad you found me. This is the cookbook that will satisfy your craving.

How to use this book

In writing *The Marketing Cookbook for Translators*, I wanted to create an easy to follow guide for freelance translators looking to build or grow their business, which outlines all the marketing and client retention strategies to make that dream a reality. I wanted it to be as easy as following a recipe in a cookbook. I listened to a podcast last year that said, "What is your recipe for success? What's in your cookbook?" and that gave me the idea for this e-book.

This book is divided up into easy to follow sections. You can pick one recipe at a time, start cooking (practicing) and enjoy a delicious result.

Each recipe contains a list of ingredients, action steps, resources and further actions. If you are new to freelance translation, the inventory of your pantry and appetizers will provide lots of valuable information, while more experienced translators can jump straight to the main courses and side dishes for some tips on marketing services to your ideal clients.

Results to expect

After reading this book you will have:

- The tools to market your translation services in an efficient way
- Methods and systems to perform the marketing to your ideal clients.
- Strategies to maintain a continuous marketing plan to find new clients and keep your existing clients, and to get the word out about your translation services so that the clients can find you, instead of you trying to find them.

By following these recipes you will have a system for marketing and finding your ideal clients. You just need to do the cooking.

Before rolling up one's sleeves and getting to work, a seasoned cook always begins by taking inventory of the pantry. Becoming familiar with the tools and ingredients, as well as taking note of what needs to be picked up at the supermarket is an essential first step in any recipe. It lays the foundation for how each recipe will turn out and ensures that the chef doesn't find him or herself in a bind half way through cooking.

As an entrepreneur, it's easy to become swept away by the pressing deadlines and seemingly endless to-do lists that go along with building a business. In fact, it's tempting to run full speed ahead without ever really taking the time to slow down and observe. But when we do take the time to become curious about the skills, talents, contacts, and resources at our disposal, we're often pleasantly surprised to realize that we have a lot more to work with than we thought.

It's also possible to discover that there are some key ingredients that we are lacking. These ingredients could be specific knowledge or abilities that we will have to acquire if we hope to complete the recipe correctly. That's OK. Of course it's more fun to open the pantry door and find all the shelves fully stocked, but that is not always the reality. The important thing is to become aware of what's in the pantry and what's on the shopping list. Chances are if something is out of stock, you know exactly where to turn to fill that need.

In this chapter, we are going to explore what it takes to become a successful freelance translator and begin to become aware of what tools and ingredients you'll need to have in your kitchen. Then we will discuss the 12 most common mistakes that new freelance translators make and how you can avoid committing them yourself. Like the business world, a kitchen is full of hazards and there are infinite ways that a recipe can go awry. So how do chefs cope with the perils of the kitchen? They anticipate and adjust. They take safety precautions and learn from those around them. That's exactly what we will do together as you begin to construct your thriving translation business.

Taking this time to set the stage is what makes the difference between launching a business, and struggling to piece together a career. Are you ready to get started? Let's begin.

1.1: The Lay of the Land

Imagine that you've stepped into the kitchen at your favorite local restaurant. You look around you and see a handful of cooks in white coats chopping away, or stirring pots on the stove. They have their heads down and are hard at work on a variety of tasks. So you begin to wonder, do you really have what it takes to hold your own in a kitchen like this? And equally as important: Is this really the career that is right for you?

At one point or another, professionals in every industry across the board will face these same doubts. They can be uncomfortable and difficult to face, but if you tackle them early on in the game, you'll save yourself from having to make a U-turn later down the line.

In order to decide whether or not you have the skills and passion to succeed as a translator, you're going to have to better understand the translation industry. Contrary to popular opinion, not everyone who speaks more than one language can become (or should become) a translator. So the question is: What exactly does it take to achieve success in this competitive field? Based on my experience, here are the characteristics that distinguish the "top chefs" of translation:

Excellent skills in your native language

Professional translators always translate into their native language. For that reason, excellent writing skills are essential. Successful translators have a strong understanding of grammar as well as knowledge of different language variations.

Only if you are completely bilingual in a second language should you venture into translating into a language that is not your native tongue. Keep in mind that your translations will likely be read by native speakers who will easily recognize language flaws and often have vast experience in a specific field. The general recommendation is that if you cannot match the writing level with that of your readers, then you are not equipped to write professional texts in that language.

Bilingual

Not only should translators have near-perfect language skills in their native tongue, they should also exhibit near-native proficiency in the source language(s) of the texts that will undergo translation. Understanding the nuances of what you are translating will help you find the right words to ensure that the original meaning remains intact.

Vast cultural knowledge

Language is dynamic, and changes through both time and space. Cultivating a depth of cultural knowledge (in both the target and source language locales), allows you to craft more accurate translations. The truth is that people in different communities use language differently. They think differently and have different stimuli and value systems, each of which are reflected in the vocabulary and grammar that they use. Successful translators stay tuned in to these linguistic variations.

An area of expertise

Because quality translations rely on depth of knowledge and linguistic precision, specializing in 1-2 subjects can provide a huge competitive advantage.

Rather than trying to learn a little bit about everything, specialization allows you to focus your energies only on the areas that you are most passionate about or that are likely to provide the greatest return. Ideally you should be able to comfortably discuss the subject matter with the author of the original text. That means familiarizing yourself with the concepts and technical jargon of that specific topic.

But how should you go about choosing a specialization? Your best bet is to choose an area of expertise from your previous job history, if possible. If you have not worked in other industries, that's OK, too. It simply means that you're going to need to tap into your social network to find someone who has. Perhaps a close friend or family member specializes in a particular field – such as electrical engineering, or

Education and Law

pediatric medicine – and would be willing to be your mentor.

Translators that are new to the business often resist the advice to "narrow down" their work to one or two specialties. That's understandable. It can feel limiting and give the sensation that you are turning your back on opportunities. However, choosing the right specialization can be the one decision that brings in a steady stream of opportunities and clients. Targeting a specific area (or niche market) allows you to concentrate your efforts and provide higher quality and efficiency.

It will also make it easier to identify and communicate with your target audience, allowing you to speak directly to a group of people rather than marketing to anyone within earshot. I know several translators who specialize in very narrow subjects, such as cosmetics or waste management, and they do very well for themselves. They can speak directly to a special target group, and they have the knowledge to be able to discuss subjects with clients in detail. The clients view them as valuable experts – and that is the greatest advantage of all. When you are seen as a valuable expert or specialist within a specific field, your rates naturally begin to rise.

Customer service and friendliness

Freelance translators are essentially entrepreneurs, and as a result, they are required to fulfill many roles outside of merely producing translations. True, a great deal of your time will be spent at the keyboard, but you will also have to manage client relations and customer service on a daily basis. Handling customer contact with professionalism and friendliness is essential to retaining clients for long-term business.

Powers of negotiation

Because you will be wearing many hats as a freelance translator, at times you will be working in sales and bill collection. Negotiating prices and collecting payment can be uncomfortable moments even for the smoothest talkers among us. However, with a few negotiation skills, you will be able to establish fair prices confidently and effectively.

Self-motivation

Freelancers are their own bosses, and therefore they are responsible for their own time management day in and day out. As a freelance translator you will need to be self-motivated and highly disciplined in order to make sure that daily tasks are done on time and with the highest quality possible. You will also need to establish a balance between servicing existing clients and performing the strategic planning tasks necessary to manage and grow your business. This includes creating and executing a solid business plan as well as performing the necessary marking tasks along the way.

Marketing skills

Freelance translators often tremble at the idea of having to take charge of marketing their personal brand. However, an effective marketing plan is what attracts a steady stream of clients to your business, and allows you to enjoy a sustainable income year in and year out. Having some marketing knowledge (and chances are you know more than you think you do) will help you clarify your business goals, identify your ideal customers, and communicate with them in compelling ways.

It's easy to feel that without an MBA or a fancy marketing degree, building a business is nothing more than an uphill battle. Thankfully, that's really not the case. (Later in this book we'll explore the marketing techniques you can use to boost your business – without ever going back to school.)

Tech savvy

Basic IT skills are necessary to ensure that the day-to-day business runs smoothly. It's helpful to know how a computer works, how to conduct online research, and how to leverage online marketing tools. Today, the majority of translators work with a computer-aided translation tool, or CAT tool, which also requires some technical skills in order to benefit from all the functions.

Formal education

Though a formal degree is certainly not a prerequisite, a university degree, and/or a qualification in translation – such as a certification or a degree – can help to prove your expertise and make you more competitive when applying for jobs as a freelance translator. Most translators hold advanced degrees in areas other than translation, and that's perfectly fine. Chances are you'll find that whatever you studied in college or graduate school, will – in some unexpected way – become useful in your translation business.

It's not a requirement to possess every skill in this list before starting a translation business; however they do represent some of the most important abilities necessary to become a successful freelancer. If you've found that you have a few of these skills, but are missing several others, don't worry. Many skills can be quickly acquired and often at very little cost. There are many courses available that can quickly improve your skills in, for example, writing, keyboarding, CAT tools, business and marketing skills.

However, other abilities are not quite so easy to come by. If you find that you are not an excellent linguist, or lack self-motivation and organization, your career as a freelance translator could be rather difficult. Skills can be learned and habits can be cultivated, but if you find that you lack many characteristics on the list or doubt that translation is your passion, you may be better suited for a different vocation.

1.2: Twelve Common Mistakes

 After you've taken inventory of your pantry and have confirmed that a career as a translator is the right path for you, it's time to take a closer look at what that road looks like – and some of the potholes you're likely to encounter along the way. After more than 10 years in the business, I am a firm believer that some of the most valuable insights come from those who have gone before us. In this section we are going to discuss some of the most common mistakes that translators make during the early stages of their businesses.

If, as you read through this list, you realize that you've already fallen into a number of these potholes, don't feel guilty! I know that I myself have committed one or two of these mistakes. The important thing is to recognize that each of these errors offers learning, and as soon as you become aware that you've slipped into a pothole, simply take action to put your business back on track as quickly as possible.

#1 - Not choosing a specialization

It's important to decide early on to focus your efforts on a subject matter or field that you are good at. You may already have expertise in a field from a previous career or perhaps from a college degree program. Your experience may offer you the chance to specialize in areas such as medical translation, computer technology, law, engineering, design and the arts, or something in between. If you really don't feel that you have any expertise in a particular field, then it's time to go out and get some. You can try to gain some relevant in-house experience in a particular area, or complete an accredited course to demonstrate competence to potential clients. Avoid the temptation to add a dozen subjects to your list of specializations in an attempt to get more jobs. This completely defeats the point, and it will only damage your credibility. By choosing a niche, you can become an authority on the subject you choose and the go-to-resource for your clients.

#2 - Starting out with very low rates

Setting rates for translation services is never easy, and it's often very tempting early in your career to set very low rates in an attempt to gain more experience. However, this is a strategy that's likely to come back and bite you later on down the road. Low rates can devalue your service offer and give the wrong impression – communicating to your clients that you are too new to the game, or that your translation services are not high quality. A better strategy is to offer free test translations to gain a client's confidence, or reduce charges for supplementary services such as proofreading or testing. Do your research, calculate what you need to earn to make a decent living and set appropriate rates that will allow you to be taken seriously. I will discuss rate calculation in a later chapter in this book.

#3 - Being afraid to ask questions

Many new translators are afraid to ask questions of their clients when receiving a new project, fearing that the client will be turned off and suspect that the translator doesn't know what he or she is doing. I can testify that this is not the case! If your questions are intelligent, and will assist you in providing a higher quality product in the end, your clients will appreciate you taking the time to ask. Clients value translators who make sure they understand the task and the text before diving into the work. Find out the intended purpose of the translation and the target audience. Ask for clarification of words that may be difficult to understand. Just make sure you ask relevant questions (well in advance of the deadline).

#4 - Not belonging to a professional organization

My career took off when I joined the American Translators Association. A membership in a professional organization will set you apart from the hobby translators and will give you credibility by showing that you fulfill the organization's standards. In addition, many of these organizations offer numerous opportunities for networking, continuing education and personal development.

#5 – Not setting up good accounting practices and saving for taxes

Treat your business professionally from the start. Have a separate account for your business and keep track of all your income and expenses. This can be done in a spreadsheet or by using any of the accounting tools available on the market today. I use QuickBooks, since I have now outsourced my accounting, but many translators are also very happy with Translation Office 3000. If you hate accounting, you might want to invest in a professional accountant as soon as you can afford it. Another good idea is to put approximately 20-30% of all payments away for tax purposes right away, to make sure you have the money to pay the taxes after you file your first income return.

#6 - Not researching new clients before working with them

Another strong temptation is to accept every new client that contacts you, particularly early in your career when you are hungry for experience and eager to begin building your business. Resist this urge! Not all clients are created equal. You will find that there are a number of people who will try to take advantage of new freelancers by requesting free services, or you may run into unprofessional agencies that will not respect your prices or payment plan. When a new client contacts you, you should always make sure to request their full company name and address, and visit their website. Secondly, invest in PaymentPractices.net, the oldest and most extensive dataset related to the payment practices of translation agencies and other consumers of translation services. Another resource for checking out a new client is the Blue Board from ProZ.com. You can do a search of the new agency and see what other people say about their payment history. Evaluate every client that contacts you the same way that you would evaluate a potential employee. After all, you will be working closely with this person or organization and you don't want to find yourself in the midst of a bad relationship with nothing to show for your hard work at the end of the day.

#7 - Being afraid of turning down a project

I have also found that many new translators are afraid to turn projects down, thinking they might lose the client. I remember that when I first started out in the industry, I translated some marketing materials for a blowtorch, thinking that I could do it because I knew marketing lingo. Little did I know that blowtorches have very specialized words and use common words differently. It was a nightmare project and I did not produce a good quality translation –

and boy did I hear about it from the proofreader! Though it was highly uncomfortable at the time, it is a lesson that I will never forget.

New freelancers also tend to accept all sorts of projects just to gain experience, but if you are not 100% confident that you know the subject and the text, then you should not accept the job. If you take on a project that you cannot translate well, or accept a deadline that you cannot meet, you will only damage your relationship with the client. Most clients respect and appreciate it if you turn down a project if you believe you cannot do a good job, and they will keep you in mind for future projects down the road.

#8 - Not prioritizing marketing and networking

It is not enough to register a profile in a translator database and wait for the projects to come to you. In today's competitive marketplace, it is important to set aside time for continuous marketing and networking so that clients can find you easily. Create a website, join one or two social media networks, attend conferences, join professional associations and attend business networking events to make people aware of your services. **The simple truth of freelancing is that people cannot hire you if they cannot find you.** They can't refer work to you if they don't know who you are.

Often people imagine networking to be this scary, inaccessible thing – but the truth is, you already have a network of people surrounding you that you have likely not tapped into. Begin networking with your friends, family, and colleagues. The most successful translators are the ones that support their colleagues and share valuable information. Because many translators work from home offices, our work environments tend to be somewhat isolated from the rest of the work. That's why it's so important to get out of your office and meet other translators or clients. People prefer to work with people they know and trust and the time you spend networking can be a good investment that leads to future collaborations.

I do not think of other Swedish translators as competitors, but as colleagues and potential collaborators. There is enough translation work out there for all of us, if we just go out of our way to find it.

#9 - Poor communication with clients

There is nothing worse for a project manager or client than having to deal with uncertainty. Clients don't want to spend their time staring at the computer screen thinking: Will she deliver the project in time? Did he get the last email with the updated text? Can she open the file? Don't let clients worry about these things. Make sure you respond to emails promptly, acknowledge receipt of each correspondence, and follow their instructions. Let clients know that they can rely on you and the client will want to come back to you with work time and time again.

Make it a habit to keep in touch with your clients regularly, and not only when you need work. Let them know when you are on vacation. Inform them of new courses you have taken, or new CAT tools (computer aided translation tools) that you are currently working with. If your customers ask for updated information, make sure you respond promptly.

Lastly, don't forget to ask for references. Word of mouth and recommendations are your most powerful marketing tools – and a tool that most new translators forget to use. Make it a habit each time you complete a project to ask for feedback, especially when you first start out, and ask for permission to publish this feedback as a testimonial. You may decide to create a free survey using tools such as Survey Monkey or Google Doc Forms. Then, email a survey link out to every client when you finish each project. Use their feedback to polish your services, your business processes, and publish the powerful testimonials on your website to capture new clients.

#10 - Not prioritizing professional development

The translation industry is constantly changing and developing, with new processes and new tools becoming available every day. That's why it's important to keep current with changes and not resist learning new tools. Stay on top of new technology as well as your areas of specialization, and consider investing in additional education or professional development programs. Though courses, certifications, trainings, and development programs will all require an investment of time and money, they are essential investments that must be made if you have any hope to stay on top of your game and the market. Not to mention that a well-placed investment in yourself will likely more than pay for itself in new clients and opportunities.

#11 - Having unrealistic goals when first starting out

The early stages of building a freelance translation business can be frustrating. Many beginning freelancers are disappointed that they are not receiving any jobs even if they have applied to 40 agencies or clients. It usually takes several hundred applications before you can find your first good clients. Don't expect to become a successful translator in a few months; 6 months to a year is a much more realistic time frame for your business to truly take shape and to start generating sustainable income. Most translators reach a satisfying stream of clients and income around three years after starting their business.

#12 – Underestimating the effort required

Being a freelancer is a lot of work. Unlike a regular 9 to 5 check-in-check-out job, in the world of freelance translation there is always something you can improve on, always more you can do to grow your business. I am not saying that you should always work. It is also important to create a work-life balance that you can both sustain and enjoy. At the same time, it is important to realize that your translation business will require a lot of effort and dedication, but most of the time, it is worth it to become your own boss and take full responsibility for your own future.

 Resources:
Ten typical mistakes start-up freelance translators should avoid, By Nicole Y. Adams.

7 Mistakes Freelance Translators Should Avoid, by Levent Yildizgoren.

1.3: Choosing Specializations

In section 1 we briefly discussed why it is important to choose a specialization. We discussed that focusing in on 1-2 areas of expertise allows you to show mastery of a particular subject matter, while at the same time helping you to identify who your target audience is, so that you can speak directly to them in all of your marketing and communications efforts.

Online competition can be steep, and choosing a specialization is your most powerful opportunity to stand out from the crowd. A technical translator and a literary translator have completely different skill sets, even if they both work with translation. If you want to work with a variety of direct clients, there is plenty of available work in practically any specialization you can think of. However, if you want to work with agencies, you have to target one of their specialties, which most likely include financial, medical, legal, pharmaceutical, IT and patents.

So how should you go about choosing a specialization?

1. Base it on your previous experience.
    Many translators have had a previous career. They may be doctors or lawyers who got tired of their everyday tasks and have decided to become translators who specialize in medical or legal texts, incorporating their previous professional experience. For example, my education is in marketing and I have worked with IT companies, which is why I chose to specialize in these two areas when I first began my translation business. Many subject matters in translation require the kind of expertise that only people who have worked in the field can possess. Becoming an expert within a particular industry often requires years of study or experience, so if you already have previous experience, you are already ahead.

2. Pick an area that you enjoy researching.
    Working within a specific specialization or industry requires that you learn that topic inside and out. You'll likely conduct your own research, read trade publications, network with

industry insiders, and you may even take educational classes related to the topic you choose. Given the hours of investigation that go into making you an expert in your field, it's important to choose a subject that interests you. If you don't feel passionate – or at the very least, highly curious – about the subject matter, chances are you're not going to have the motivation to become a true specialist.

3. Know what you don't want to do.
   When choosing your specialization, it's just as important to know what topics you want to learn inside and out, and what topics you wouldn't touch with a ten-foot pole. Weed out the subject matters that you have no interest in learning or would likely never feel competent translating. In my case, I decided to eliminate legal translations and patents. I do not have any legal experience and, to me, many legal texts are difficult to read and just plain boring (but that is my personal opinion).

4. Follow the money.
   Yes, choosing a specialization that interests you is important, but it's also important that you choose one that can support your business

and your lifestyle. This point does not exclude the previous ones, but it is worth considering all the same. If you specialize in an industry that does not have a high need for translation in your languages or that does not have money to pay for translations, it will not be profitable. It is wise to focus on an industry (law, IT, pharmaceuticals) in which clients must translate texts in order to do business with other countries and cultures. It is also wise to focus on an industry (corporate communications, hospitality, tourism) where clients hope that a good translation will bring them more business and profits. Do a little online research and interview professionals within the business to get a better idea of just how much demand exists within a particular industry.

5. Consider your interests and hobbies. Our natural tendency is to learn more about the subjects that we are interested in. We learn the ins and outs of our hobbies and become familiar with the jargon of topics that interest us. For example, I could probably translate yoga material quite well since I have practiced yoga in both the US and Sweden, and I love

reading about it. I am also fairly well versed in nutrition and could make this an area of expertise if I really wanted to. Robot building or Web analytics? Not so much.

Some tips on specializations:

- **Completing one project is not the same as choosing a specialization.** Just because you have experience in a field from a few projects does not mean that you are ready to promote yourself as an expert within that field. In order to reach specialization status, you are going to need to cultivate in-depth knowledge within a particular area of study. Completing a degree program or several years of work experience is enough to earn you a specialization. Translating a single project or picking up a trade magazine is not.

- **The more specialized your language combination, the less specialized your area of expertise needs to be.** If you've spent any amount of time in the translation world, you know that some language combinations are in higher demand than others. The more specialized your language combinations are, the less specialized you will need to be in the subject matter that you focus on. However, if your language combinations are not rare, you will need to select a specific niche or industry. Freelance translators who specialize early in their careers are able to more effectively market their services and distinguish themselves from a sea of online translators.

- **Embrace continuing education in your specialization.** Once you have chosen a specialization, you can improve your skills in the field by taking educational courses, either online or at a local university. For example, Coursera.org offers numerous free courses in specialist subjects for the public. You can sign up for them, complete them online, and even receive a certificate when you successfully complete the class.

- **Read as much as you can on the subject.** A wealth of information is available online 24/7 at your fingertips, but the Internet is not your only source of information on your specialty subject. You can also subscribe to a number of trade journals that are published specifically for professionals within a particular field.

Trade publications will provide you with interesting feature articles about new developments, technologies, trends, and projects within an industry. Journals will also showcase manufacturers and suppliers that you may be able to contact as potential translation clients. New clients will love to see that you are keeping a finger on the pulse of their industry and you're up-to-date with the latest developments taking place in their field.

- **Collect terminology and build glossaries or term bases for your special fields.** If you put some work into developing translation memories and glossaries, you will gradually be able to complete your projects faster and with a higher degree of accuracy. The more you are able to streamline your translation process within a particular subject matter, and deliver quality that stands out amongst the competition, the more profitable your business, and the more clients you are able to work with.

- **Look for workshops both online and in your local area** to gain knowledge and understanding of your subject matter. Live events and workshops are also great for networking with other translators that you could potentially collaborate with, as well as making contact with potential clients.

- **Find experts that can help you expand your knowledge.** An expert could be someone working in the industry you specialize in, or an experienced translator with a similar language combination who is willing to help mentor you or proofread your work until you begin to build more confidence. Client retention always hinges on your ability to provide excellent quality translations. For that reason, it may be worth paying an expert to proofread your work in the early stages of your business, ensuring that every client is satisfied, and helping you learn the ins and outs of your niche.

- **Stand out as a specialist in your local area** by networking. Make a constant effort to attend trade shows in your specific field and gather together a team of experts in your niche. You can also position yourself as an expert in your field by publishing articles or blog posts in your areas of specialization.

Resources:

Choosing Your Translation Specializations, by Corinne McKay (www.thoughtsontranslation.com).

Why Specialization in Language Translation Matters, from Translatorsbase.com.

Specializing, from ProZ.com Wiki

1.4: Buying Training Ingredients

Some of you are still studying, or have just graduated with a degree in translation. Others have started translation as a second career, with education and/or work experience from other fields. No matter where you come from, it is important to focus on training and continuing education as a translator.

If you already have a degree in translation, you will likely need additional business knowledge and marketing skills that will help you build the foundation of your freelance career and continuously attract a steady stream of clients and income. If however, you do not have a degree in translation, but you already specialize in an area of study, you will need to bolster up your language skills. This may come in the form of learning translation techniques and/or proofreading and editing skills, among others.

In my experience, the important thing is to be aware of what skills you have and what skills you need to acquire. Doing so requires embracing a life and career of constant study and improvement. Every translator benefits immensely from learning to use new translation tools and technology. I would even go so far as to say that it is necessary to know how to use a CAT tool and have a full understanding of how machine translation works.

However, every translator is different, and some have a great aptitude for learning, while others need to push themselves in order to incorporate new techniques. In this section we will focus on filling the gaps in your translation pantry and equipping you with all the resources, skills, and gadgets necessary to take your translation business to the next level.

Translator Training Resources

- **Local and national translation associations**
  Translation associations provide many excellent educational opportunities for translators, both in person and sometimes also as webinars. Some large and well-known national translator associations include the American Translators Association and the Institute of Translators and Interpreters in the UK, which also accepts members worldwide.

- **Professional trade associations**
  Joining professional trade groups in your specialist area will also open you up to many educational opportunities as well as the opportunity to easily network with a sea of potential clients.

- **Online Courses**
  MOOC providers (Massive Open Online Courses) such as Coursera provide online classes at the university level on almost any imaginable topic. These courses are generally available for very low prices and many are entirely free. Some even offer a certificate at the

end of the course for students who successfully complete all requirements.

- **eCPD Webinars**
  This independent organization provides online training courses for translators and interpreters. These webinars and courses focus on continuing professional development for anyone who wants to hone their skills in the art of translation, the business of translation, and translation and interpreting technology. (www.ecpdwebinars.co.uk)

- **Alexandria Online Translation Resources**
  This is also an independent organization that provides online workshops, online courses or webinars for translators, interpreters or translation companies, both live and on demand. (www.alexandria-translation-resources.com

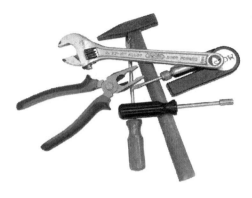

By now you have a pretty good idea of what skills and knowledge will be necessary to take your translation business to the next level, but it's time to get down to the nuts and bolts of building up your business. For that job, you're going to need a number of different tools to become a thriving freelance translator. Here is your shopping list:

- **A good computer**

  A reliable computer that you feel comfortable using is the cornerstone of your translation business. For example, I have a desktop computer in my office and a laptop for when I'm on the road. It's also wise to have a backup computer in case your main computer ever crashes, which happens more frequently than you may think.

- **A fast and secure Internet connection**

  Virtual communication with your clients and colleagues is critical, and anytime your Internet connection goes out, you drop off the map and leave your clients wondering if their projects are going to be completed on time. Having reliable access to the Web will also allow you to research and market your services throughout the day.

- **A backup system for your work**

  You do not have to fear losing many hours of work anymore, or losing whole documents due to a system crash. The options for backing up your work are numerous. You may decide to back up your information in the cloud, on a portable hard disk, or both – as long as you consistently create a copy of your files on two separate storage devices, either choice is completely valid. I prefer to use Dropbox.com as my primary backup system. I have even set it up so that it backs up my files and synchronizes continuously from my desktop computer, my laptop, and my smartphone. I no longer have to schedule backups into my planner, or feel the panic when I forget to protect my files. Very rarely there are special circumstances when client confidentiality is so strict that the client does not want any files stored encrypted in the cloud. In these cases, I simply save them in a separate file on my computer hard drive and back them up manually onto an external hard drive. The question of how often to back up your work is one that you will have to answer for yourself.

- **A reference library of professional dictionaries**

  Stock your office with professional libraries in your source and target languages. These can be in paper format or electronic format on your computer or online, whichever you prefer. However, it is important not to rely too heavily on the Internet and Google to help you out when you are stuck on a particular term. I use Wordfinder and have downloaded general dictionaries and specialist dictionaries, grammatical guidelines, synonym dictionaries, and writing tips – all of which can be found in Wordfinder (www.wordfinder.com).
  .

- **A CAT tool (a computer aided translation tool)**

  If you haven't already begun using a CAT tool,

this is soon to become one of your most essential tools. A computer aided translation tool allows you to input the source text and translate it in segments at a time. The tool saves each segment in memory, which aids you in creating consistent terminology in your translations and helps you become more efficient, never having to translate the same sentence twice. The system will recognize a sentence or word you have translated before and will automatically translate for you. Some popular translation tools are Trados Studio, MemoQ, Wordfast and DejaVu. I recommend trying one or two of them out and deciding which tool works best for you.

- **A printer**
  Even if you are fiercely dedicated to a paperless lifestyle, the time will come sooner or later when you simply need to push print. You may need to have a hard copy of an agreement to sign, or you may have to print out the final draft of a text for proofreading.

- **A scanner**
  Though not absolutely essential, access to a scanner can greatly facilitate several tasks that

are likely to come up. You may need to scan a signed document to send to a customer, or scan receipts, diplomas, and documents to keep on digital file. Just keep in mind that all your scanned documents should be backed up in a second location.

- **Accounting software**
  Even at the early stages of your translation business, you'll need access to some form of accounting software to keep track of your day-to-day income and expenses. If you're interested in keeping this simple, setting up a finance tracker in Excel is a low-budget and easy-to-use option. However, if you want to go professional and organized, I highly recommend the following tools:
  - QuickBooks (if you want to hire an accountant, most of them use this).
  - Translation Office 3000 (easy to use and especially developed for translators) (www.translation3000.com).

Of course, hiring your own accountant to do your taxes and book keeping is another viable option, though it comes at a slightly higher cost.

Congratulations!

If you've made it this far that means that you've fully stocked your pantry with all the knowledge, convictions, and tools to start cooking up your translation success.

You've examined the primary characteristics of successful freelance translators and compared them to your own skills and knowledge to determine whether this is truly the right career for you. Then you took a look at the lay of the land and learned about the 12 most common potholes that translators fall into on the road to building thriving businesses, and you also acquired some foolproof strategies for avoiding those pitfalls.

Then you faced perhaps the biggest indicator of your future success: narrowing down your focus into 1-2 specializations. Hopefully by this point you have a fairly clear idea of what you would like to specialize in, or at least have a few ideas of subject areas worthy of a little more investigation. I know it feels counterintuitive to narrow down your focus, particularly if you're in the growing stages of your business when you feel hungry for just any old client to walk through your door. But trust me. My experience has taught me that positioning yourself as a known expert within a niche will open up the client floodgates, nourishing your business with high quality clients for years to come.

Chapter 2
Appetizers

 With a fully stocked pantry and large dose of know-how, you're finally ready to get down to work in your business-building kitchen. Now that you already have the translation skills and tools you need, it's time to start turning your services into a real business. After all, if customers can't find you, you have no way of providing your service and making an income.

That's what we'll focus on in this chapter: the foundations of your marketing strategy. In my experience, most translators get a little nervous when the 'marketing' word enters the conversation. It may be new territory, it may require you to learn new processes, new skills, new knowledge – but that's what I'm here to teach you.

It all starts with a recipe. Without reading the recipe first and initially planning your dish, you are likely to end up leaving out key ingredients or botching important steps. The same is true for your marketing. If you have a plan, and know what steps you'll have to take and the order you'll have to take them in, suddenly everything becomes much easier.

In this chapter we will explore the appetizer recipes, all the foundational planning of your marketing efforts. Take the time to go through this chapter carefully and you'll be sure to lay a strong foundation for the marketing efforts that will soon funnel clients through your door. Even as an experienced translator, I regularly go back to the foundations to tweak my services and analyze my goals and strengths.

 Recipe 1: *Your Business Foundation*

 Laying the foundation of your business is perhaps the most fundamental step and is, ironically, one that too many business owners rush through. Whether you've

already started your translation business or are just beginning to market your services, I encourage you to take the time to work through this section as thoughtfully as you possibly can.

You may have begun piecing together a vision for what you would like your business to be in the future. But chances are you have done all this powerful vision work in your head and not on paper. That's fine, but until you get out of your head and onto paper, it is going to be extremely difficult for you to take action and begin construction.

Studies have shown that when we physically write down our goals and desires on paper, the chances of actually achieving what we want increase dramatically. Therefore, even if you've already thought about it, even if you've already begun to take action, I invite you to set aside 1-2 hours of time to complete some important questions.

Ingredients

- Analysis of your current situation.
- Pen and paper, whiteboard or mindmap.

The following questions may require you to do a little research, to critically consider the reality of your business, the reality of your market, and the reality of what you want as a business owner. Feel like you're ready? Let's dig in!

Steps

Answer the following questions:

- **What services do you offer?**
    - What are the products or services that you already offer or hope to offer to your clients?
    - How are your services or products priced and how are they differentiated from each other?

- **What areas do you specialize in?**
    - What topics, industries, niches, or subject matter are you already an expert in?
    - If you do not already have a specialty, what areas would you like to specialize in and what steps do you need to take to build your expertise?

- What areas do you believe have a strong demand for translation services in your language set?

• **Who are your clients?**

If you are marketing to businesses, consider what industry your clients work in, the size and nature of their businesses, their geographical location, and the needs that you will fulfill. If you have more than one specialty, you may find that you have several different client groups. In that case, prioritize your audiences by ranking them from most important to least important. You may be able to serve all of them, but your marketing efforts will be designed to focus on the most lucrative clientele.

• **Who are your competitors?**

This question may require you to do some online research. If you are not already aware of the top five companies competing for a space in your niche market, simply conduct some online searches. Find out the business' names, the services/product portfolio they offer, the size of their market share, their prices, their brand messaging and positioning.

This is also an excellent time to take notes on what they are doing that you are not, and create a short to-do list of things you would like to incorporate into your business.

You can also take notes on things your competition may be missing out on. Perhaps you notice a service they don't offer, or a client group they ignore.

Ask yourself: What opportunities are they not taking advantage of?

- **What are your unique selling points?**

Now that you have a sense of who your ideal clients are and what your competition is already offering, it's time to find out where you fit in the mix.
  - What do you offer that sets you apart from the crowd? What differentiates your business?

- Is it your services/ product portfolio, your price points, customer service, reliability, turnaround speed, language set, specialty, branding?

Knowing what makes you different (and better) than the rest will help you know what messages to emphasize in your marketing efforts. You'll want to make it easy for customers to recognize what makes you different and understand why that makes you better than the other companies serving your niche.

If you are unclear on this point, turn to the people that already have the answer: your past clients! Ask them why they chose your company, what stood out to them, and how you compare to any previous translators they may have worked with in the past. If you're a little nervous about asking for this feedback, just remember that your clients (particularly repeat clients) already support your business and if you approach them professionally they will likely be more than happy to help.

Resources:

The Business Guide For Translators, by Marta Stelmaszak, 2014.

Recipe 2: *SMART Goals*

First of all it's important to be clear about what your primary goal is. What do you want to achieve in your business? For freelance translators, there are basically three ways to grow your business. You can:

1. Raise your prices
2. Find new clients
3. Sell more to existing clients

A clear goal is the first thing you need to have when building your marketing strategy. Perhaps you'll decide to focus on one of the three options in the list above, or perhaps you'll decide you need to do all three. If you decide that your business is in need of all three, that's completely valid. However, in my experience I have found that business owners who try to tackle all three at once wind up overwhelming themselves and successfully achieving none of them. Therefore, focus on one thing at a time and make it a goal. Then, once you've accomplished the first one, move on to two and three.

Ingredients

- Goals for your business

Steps

One of the best marketing strategies I have ever come across is to create what are known as SMART goals. SMART goals are now used in almost every marketing book and are not only smart goals per se, but to break it down, the smart goals are:

- **S**pecific
- **M**easurable
- **A**ttainable
- **R**elevant
- **T**ime-bound

Use these criteria to define your goals and then break them down into smaller goals, each of which builds towards a larger goal. Now let's take a moment to explore each aspect of a SMART goal.

1. *Specific*

When you make your goal specific, and clearly outline exactly what is involved, it becomes more tangible and your chances of achieving it go way up. It can be very tempting to simply have a vague idea of what your business needs, but think of a specific goal like a point on a map. If your goal is highly specific, you know exactly what to put into your GPS and you can find a way to walk straight to the front door. However, if your goal is undefined, you're not going to know which roads to take and you have no way of knowing whether or not you've arrived.

To make a goal tangible and specific, try asking yourself the following questions and write your answers down:

- Who: Who is involved?
  Who are the companies or people in the companies you are trying to target?

- What: What exactly do I want to accomplish? If you say to yourself, "I want to gain more clients", exactly how many new clients per month would you like to sign on? How many new clients per year?

- Where: Is there a location involved in the goal? Will your work take place on your website, on a specific location online, in your town, in a different region, or in a foreign country?

- When: What is the specific time frame for this goal?
  When does it absolutely need to be completed by? If it's not necessarily time sensitive, when would you like to have it completed by? What is the ideal deadline and what is the hard-and-fast deadline?

- Why: Why do I need to achieve this goal? Be sure to get clear about the specific reasons, purpose or benefits of accomplishing this goal. If you do not know why you want to achieve a goal, it may be because it is simply not important enough for your business. Dig deep for your reason why and if you come up short simply try a different goal.

Here is an example of how your goal can transform from vague to specific.

Vague: "I want to get more clients next year."

Specific: "In January am going to use LinkedIn to start following other professionals and create interactions with five companies that I would like to work with in order to achieve 10 new clients in 20XX."

2. *Measurable*

Make the goal measurable by finding criteria to measure your success along the way. If you can find a way to measure your goal, you'll be able to track your progress, adjust your actions to create greater improvement, and fuel yourself with motivation to continue working towards the finish line.

To determine if your goal is measureable, ask yourself some of the following questions:

1. How much?
2. How many?
3. How will I know when it is accomplished?

For example, in how many days, weeks, months; how many contacts, how much money? You'll need to set a specific metric for measuring your progress.

3. *Attainable*

If your goal is too unrealistic or impossible to attain, you will find motivation very hard to come by. Remember, you want to set goals that are actually possible to attain from where you are today – so don't set goals for some future self – set goals unique to you and your business. That is not to say that you shouldn't set your sights high, because you should, but you also need to break them down into smaller goals and steps that you can regularly take to move your business forward.

It's possible for you to attain almost any goal, but only if you plan your steps and establish a time frame for performing them. If you find that you've selected an overwhelming (though realistic) goal, you'll be surprised by just how motivated you will become when you break it down into steps. Here is a question to help you get started.

- How can the goal be accomplished?

4. *Relevant*

For a goal to work for you it needs to be relevant for your business. That means that it should be a goal that advances your business and that you are willing and motivated to work towards. If you set up a goal that you do not care about, or that you do not think is important for your business in the long term, chances are your motivation will be slim.

A relevant goal should answer yes to the following questions:

- Does this goal seem worthwhile?
- Is this the right direction for me and my business to go after this outcome?
- Is this goal in line with the kind of work I want to be doing, or does it take me off on a tangent and distract me from my true mission?
- Am I the right person to tackle this goal or will I need to find collaborators to ensure that I succeed? If I need collaborators, who should I reach out to?

For example, a relevant goal for me was to hire an accountant to outsource my tax management and accounting, because I am not good at doing it myself, and thus not motivated to do it. Accounting takes up too much of my time that would better be spent translating or focusing on acquiring new clients.

5. *Time-bound*

The final qualification for your goal to be SMART is that your goal should be time-bound, meaning that it needs to have a timeline and a deadline. If your goal is not attached to any date on a calendar, you'll find that it is simply too easy to procrastinate or put off for later. Even though you may not want to, it's important to prevent your goals from being clouded out by the day-to-day tasks of your business. Therefore, set a deadline and work your way backwards by setting milestone deadlines and a time frame that you feel comfortable completing.

A time-bound goal will usually answer the following questions:

- When do I need to begin on this goal and when do I need to complete it?
- What can I do six months from now?
- What can I do six weeks from now?
- What can I do today?

 **Resources**

How to Set Smart Goals (http://www.wikihow.com/Set-SMART-Goals)

Further actions

Sit down and answer these questions for the goal you have, and you will see that achieving your crucial outcomes will be much easier than you originally thought. Make some time to walk your goal through each of the SMART criteria and keep your notes in a place where you can easily turn to them. Good luck!

 Recipe 3: *SWOT Analysis*

Another great marketing tool to use before you start doing any complicated cooking is what is known as a SWOT analysis. A SWOT analysis can be used to discover the ways in which you are unique, what you can offer that no one else can and what to focus your efforts on. Based on the results of your analysis, it will become easier for you to identify your niche market and strategically target the clients who most need your services.

A SWOT analysis will help you analyze your strengths, weaknesses, opportunities and competitive threats. Take the time to examine each of these four areas and your business will benefit from numerous insights.

- **Strengths:** What are your strengths? What makes you and your business unique? What are you good at that set you apart from others?
  Translations – Education + Legal

- **Weaknesses:** What are you not so good at and what are the areas you feel like you could improve in? What do you hate doing? Where do you struggle? Do you want to outsource these tasks/services or how can you improve or strengthen them? *Interpreting*

- **Opportunities**: What opportunities exist for me and my business? Can I use some of my strengths to create a service that meets the needs in a new niche, or can I strengthen my position as a business partner among my clients? Can I partner up with other freelance translators in my field to create a strong team

75

that will better meet my clients' needs? Can I use social media to strengthen my profile and stand out among other translators?

If you're struggling to identify your opportunities, try asking yourself the following questions:

- How many of my competitors can offer this service?
- How price-sensitive is the demand for this service?
- How big of a margin will I make and how much pressure is it under?
- How easy is it for me to offer this service?

- **Threats:** What threats or competition exist for my business? Am I spreading myself too thin across a myriad of services, which makes me look like a *Jack of all trades* rather than a professional with a specific set of qualifications? Is my knowledge in my fields of expertise or translation tools up-to-date, or should I invest in continuing education to strengthen my skills in order to provide a better service to my customers?

As you conduct your first SWOT analysis, use this template to guide you. Take half an hour to sit in a quiet place and complete each section.

Objective:

	Positive	Negative
Internal	Strengths	Weaknesses
External	Opportunities Law firms ⎫ Schools ⎬ In the Colleges ⎭ area	Threats

Resources:

How can you differentiate your company in a competitive market? by Gordon Husbands (www.gala-global.com).

SWOT Analysis for Freelancers, by Alessandra Martelli (www.mtmtranslations.com).

Further actions

Based on the results of your SWOT analysis, you can then distinguish your Unique Selling Points (USP), which define how your services are unique. These are points that you should include in your marketing to potential and existing customers.

A USP could be related to satisfying customer needs or simply filling a gap in the marketplace. You will likely use your USP in the vast majority of your marketing messaging and it should succinctly communicate to your clients exactly what makes your business unique. Keep it short – no more than two sentences – and be sure that it will resonate with your target audience.

Apart from evident quality, speed, availability and technical knowledge, your USP could be related to your unique and proven knowledge of your client's business and industry. Or it may be related to your target language's country and culture. Ask yourself if there is any way you can add value to your customers, perhaps by offering cultural consultation or an additional service that you can use to sweeten the deal.

Here are some of the competitive advantages of USPs for translators:

- *Master* Having a Ph.D. in your subject matter
- Being fully bicultural
- Having in-depth knowledge of your specialization (particularly from a former profession or extensive formal study) *Education; Legal*
- Having a government clearance certification
- Delivering excellent results that can be proven.

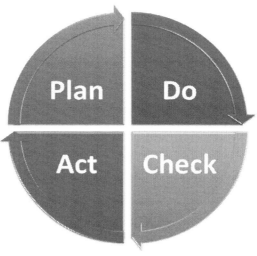

Now that we have established your SMART goals and completed your SWOT analysis, you most likely have a much better idea of what your current situation looks like, based on your strengths, weaknesses, opportunities, and competitive threats. You should also have a clearer idea of what makes you and your business unique and where your competitive advantage lies. Though it takes a little bit of effort to uncover these insights, you'll find that all of this information is crucial to help you create a plan of action that you can realistically execute.

Ingredients

Here are good things to include in your marketing plan:

- **About**: Summarize your current business situation, sales, income.
- **Goals**: Describe your goals for the next 12 months.
- **Products and Services**: Detail the products and services that you plan to offer in order to achieve your business goals. List the specifics of your offering and consider the prices that you will attach to these offerings.
- **Company specifics**: Your target market, type of company, size, location, people to contact, specialty industries
- **Marketing activities**: What marketing activities will you use to reach your goals? Calling, direct mail, applying to agencies online, contacting agencies through mail or email, LinkedIn?
- **Marketing calendar**: Plan the promotions, sales, media, and other strategies you'll use. Consider holidays and other events in your planning.

I will provide some samples of marketing or business plans so feel free to use the templates provided or mix and match their elements in order to create your own. We are all pressed for time and few professionals find themselves with several spare weeks to dedicate solely to writing out a business plan, therefore all the samples I have provided are very succinct, one-page plans that you can use as a template.

In my experience I have found that there is no need to create a lengthy business plan (that will just end up in a drawer and never be put into action). Therefore, I recommend working smarter (not harder) and pulling from a variety of other tools such as mind-maps and whiteboards to create your plan. The important thing is that you write the plan down in a way that you can easily understand. Remember, if you see your goals or tasks written down and glance at them frequently, your chances of taking action significantly increase. You may decide to do all the planning in one sitting, or to take it one part at a time – choose what works best for you. The important thing is simply to get started.

In the end you will have an easy-to-follow plan for your business' development, outlining the steps you need to take. It can even fit on one page that you can print out and post near your computer. Then it is easy to see what marketing tasks you should execute that week or month, and you will have more time and peace of mind to focus on your craft.

In order to create a relevant and well-functioning marketing plan, it's important to first define the business foundation. A freelancer also needs to be aware of his or her financial situation and financial goals.

1. The Financial Plan

 A business is not successful if it is not profitable.

Of course that sounds obvious, but you would not believe the number of business owners and freelance translators who turn a blind eye to the financial realities of their companies. I'm here to help give you the tools and guidance to create a thriving business, which means that first and foremost, you are going to have to make more money than you spend in your business. Not only will this afford you a sustainable source of income, but it will also fill you with such a sense of satisfaction and joy that will fuel you through the ups and downs of the years ahead.

Together we are going to get clear about exactly what your costs are and how much you need to make in order to pay your bills and have the financial resources to live the life you want to live. Doesn't that sound better than avoiding your bank statements as though they were the plague? Knowledge is power.

Based on the results of this simple initial analysis, you are going to be able to determine your minimum income and your desired income. This will give you the power to know where your break-even point is each month and will help you set earning goals.

1. **Get clear on your costs.**

   Make a list of all your necessary business expenses; these are the costs of keeping your business alive. Include both fixed (regular payments) and variable costs, and create a projected budget of money going out from your business each month. Be sure to include office rent payments, internet and telephone costs, office supplies, marketing costs, salaries (if you have employees or virtual assistants), web domains and hosting, memberships to professional organizations, and so on. Be as detailed as possible.

   Now do the same thing for your life. Create a list of fixed and variable costs for your personal life, which should include everything that it takes for you to live safely and happily each month. Be sure to include rent/ mortgage payments, car/ insurance/ loan payments, food, gas money, and other expenses. This will provide you with a monthly living estimate.

2. **Establish your minimum income.**

   Now add up the monthly cost of running your business and the monthly cost of living your life. This number is the absolute minimum amount you need to make each month in order to pay your bills and stay afloat.

3. **Establish your goal monthly income.**

   Chances are the budget you created in Steps 1 and 2 doesn't look like much fun. It likely doesn't leave anything extra for entertainment expenses, or savings. Don't worry; we're going to address that right now. Now it's time to go back to step 1 and create an ideal expenditure budget. Add in budgets for costs that are not absolutely essential to your survival. This may include entertainment, gym memberships, savings, travel funds, a more generous marketing budget, etc. Think about how much you would like to earn in order to not just survive, but live a lifestyle that you could really enjoy. This number represents your goal monthly income that allows you to both stay afloat and flourish.

4. **Based on these answers, what is your desired hourly, weekly, monthly annual income?** By taking the time to do these simple calculations, you are clarifying exactly what you need to charge in order to live the life you want. Rather than simply pulling your prices out of nowhere, or blindly inventing them on a whim, you will be able to justify your fees because you know exactly what you need to earn.

5. **How much do you want to work?** Perhaps the biggest benefit of becoming a freelance translator and building a business all your own, is that you are now in a position to determine – at least to some degree – how much you want to work. If you are clear on your monthly costs and ideal monthly income, but only want to work 5-7 hours a day, you may have to focus on quality projects rather than client volume.

Remember, sorting out your finances is about creating a sustainable business that you love running. Be honest with yourself about how much time you want to commit to your business and what your wants and needs are. Then adjust your plan accordingly.

 Resources:

ProZ.com's rate calculator (www.proz.com/translator-rates-calculator/).

CAL Pro – rate calculator for translators (http://www.atanet.org/business_practices/calpro_us.php).

UK version of Cal Pro (http://www.ecpdwebinars.co.uk/sitefiles/19/7/5/197552/CalPro_v1_3_EN-GB.xls).

By now you hopefully know what services you can offer your potential clients, how your services can help them, and how you are different from others offering the same translation services. You know how much you want to earn and now you can create a plan for how to achieve it.

Now it's time to dig into the tools that will allow you to make that happen. This is where we put your marketing plan into action.

If your translation business is already up and running, the idea of adding more to your to-do list can easily feel overwhelming. As business owners, particularly when we are a one-person office, it's easy to get buried beneath the day-to-day tasks of servicing clients and completing projects. I often hear translators say that it's hard to find the time and energy to focus on implementing marketing tools. I know it's hard, I have been there. But until you lift your head up from your task list, you are not going to be able to steer your company forward.

I recommend setting aside a fixed number of hours every week to focus on the business-boosting tasks that we are going to talk about in this section. Perhaps you find that you are best able to focus in the early morning hours, or later at night – whatever time you feel most inspired, set that time aside to step into your role as an entrepreneur. Aim for a minimum of 2-4 hours a week to dedicate to marketing activities and block out your schedule accordingly. One final word on this topic – do not break your marketing appointment. It can be so tempting to procrastinate, or to convince yourself that it's fine to skip because no one else will know, but don't do it. No matter how busy you are with work, do not reschedule. Your business needs your leadership; it needs you to be dedicated to marketing, because if you don't become your own marketing manager, no one else is going to take up that role.

Now, because your time is scarce and precious, it is critical that you use it wisely. How are we going to ensure you get stuff done? Easy! We are going to create a list of marketing activities that will benefit your business. That way, every time your marketing appointment rolls around, you will know exactly what you need to tackle that day.

Here are the questions you can answer to begin crafting your marketing action plan:

- How many new clients or projects do you want and in how much time?
- How much more do you want to earn?
- Where will you find your new clients?
- What marketing methods will you use? (Be as specific as possible)
- How will you market and provide service to your existing clients?
- Can you offer additional services to your existing clients?

Based on these answers, you can make a master list of marketing actions that you need to take in order to grow your business. This master list should contain every task – big and small – that you need to execute. Then, prioritize all the actions you need to take and estimate approximately how much time you need to spend on each one. Finally, plug them into a calendar of activities you can do every week and every month. If a certain action requires long-term effort, break the task into milestones and mark the milestones on your calendar as well.

Be realistic with yourself and be careful not to try to do everything all at once. Remember that professional chefs don't run around the kitchen and throw everything into the oven at the same time. Instead, they recognize that every task requires a different temperature and cook time. They plan their tasks strategically and never take on too much at once.

Follow up with yourself regularly to see what is working and what you need to change – perhaps you tried to tackle too much or too little, perhaps you noticed that your priorities were out of order. Don't be afraid to make adjustments to the calendar, and remember that it exists for your benefit. After a year it will be fun to look back at just how much your business, income and client list have changed over the course of only 12 months.

Further actions
Download or print the one page marketing plan that I have provided and use it as a template for your planning. In the coming chapters I will talk about the different methods, tools and services you can use in your marketing. Feel free to study these first before

deciding on the monthly activities and strategies for your marketing plan.

 Resources

Tess's one-page Marketing Plan for Translators (added in extra material: Checklist for Freelance Translation Marketing).

One-page business plan from 100startup.com

One-page promotional plan from 100startup.com

One of the biggest marketing challenges that any business faces is how to find and attract clients. Consider the restaurant industry. You've got a fully stocked kitchen with all the right tools, you know the head chef has honed his culinary skills, the dining room is staffed with the best employees and the ambiance is right on point. Opening night rolls around and you flip on the lights and open the front door, only to find that…nobody comes in.

You know that your food is excellent; you know that people need to eat, but still – not a single diner enters your restaurant. What's the problem? Easy, you are not on the map. You cannot help people or attract clients if people do not know your business exists. Sounds simple, but you would be shocked at just how many translators struggle to show up on their ideal clients' radar.

Now when we are ready to start talking about the actual marketing tools, we're going to start with something very basic: your resume. Even though our industry is likely to change in the coming future, for now, freelance translators still rely on the power of their resumes to land new clients and contracts, at least among agencies. Though the resume may sound like an antiquated marketing tool, it is still quite important and chances are many agency clients will ask you to send one in. You will also need to upload your resume to a variety of online databases including directories, websites. It is the easiest way for clients to evaluate your skills and today more and more people rely on online profiles to help them make hires.

Direct clients (end clients), on the other hand, are usually not interested in resumes. They are likely to search for freelance translators online, or find you through networking, or direct marketing of some kind. They are more interested in your website or brochure, which should provide them with the same information regarding your background and skills, but presented in a different format.

Because many translation agencies still rely heavily on your translation resume, it is one of the first tools you need in your marketing kitchen. Over the years I have found that many translators make the grave mistake of underestimating just how important their resume is to future clients and agencies. They don't take the time to craft a polished resume and as a result, they miss out on a massive amount of business and opportunities.

In the case of most freelance linguists, a resume is a one to two-page summary of their relevant skills, experience, and education. Because clients and recruiters receive an overwhelming amount of resumes and applications, you will want to keep your resume brief and to the point. Typical readers spend less than a minute skimming through each resume (sometimes even less), so you will need to be highly strategic about what content you include and how your information is formatted. A successful resume is concise, compelling, and contains only relevant, up-to-date information.

Here are some reasons why prospective translation clients might ask you for a resume/CV. Your resume:

- Facilitates the decision process
- Presents your qualifications in a familiar, professional format
- May be required for quality processes or procedures

Follow this recipe for creating a compelling resume:

Ingredients

- A document no longer than 1-2 pages saved in PDF format
- Your language combination and name, saved as the file name
- Your source and target languages are indicated in the resume header, or are very visibly displayed elsewhere.
- Your specialization is listed near the top of the page
- Complete and accurate contact information
- All information is relevant for the translation industry; any superfluous experience has been removed
- Experience with CAT tools (and their specific names) is indicated (if approaching a translation agency).
- Information or experience in DTP is indicated
- Relevant association memberships, credentials, and certifications are included.

- The document has been proofread and edited numerous times by at least one other person.
- All information is up-to-date, and the document is updated often.

Ingredients to avoid

- Using color photos, word art or graphic images unless they are professional images or logos
- Including your birth date, marital status, or other personal information (particularly in the case of US resumes)
- Providing a list of all your dictionaries
- Describing your hardware and a list of standard software applications
- Leaving generic fields empty (if you are using a resume template)
- Including your prices and rates
- Using unusual fonts or format
- Using acronyms
- Lying, embellishing, or inventing credentials (always be honest)
- Submitting only hard copies (Digital resumes are searchable and are highly preferred by agencies.)

1. Before creating a resume/CV, you should consider what you want to achieve with it. You want your resume to easily demonstrate to your ideal client that you are the right person for the job. Therefore, you are likely going to need to create different versions of your resume to suit a variety of different clients and projects.

   However, the resume that you upload to online platforms (such as your website, LinkedIn profile, or directories) will need to be general enough to fit a variety of different situations. Here are some situations to consider[2]:

   - Applying for a single freelance project
   - Applying for a long-term freelance contract with a corporation or direct client
   - Applying for an in-house translation position
   - Applying for a multilingual vacancy

   Based on the client and position, you will need to adapt your CV with these different opportunities in mind.

2. *Here are some tips for writing your translator resume:*

The resume needs to be impeccable, concise and informative to make it through the clutter of other resumes. It should clearly show where you belong. It should show your specific achievements expressed in numerical values whenever possible (10,000 words a week, 30 clients, or 1,000 documents, for example). Try to quantify your achievements in ways that are quickly understood and always use context to provide further explanation. Your resume should not include any fluff or meaningless buzzwords (like *strategic, leader, results-focused*), but instead should authentically express your unique skills and qualifications.

When writing a resume, bear in mind that different countries use different terms to describe this same document. In international circles the terms "resume" and "CV" are often used interchangeably. But depending on the country your prospective client lives in, the requirements for content and format will vary greatly. For example, in the US you should never include a photograph of yourself, nor should you include personal information like your birthday or marital status. On the other hand, personal photographs and data are expected and often required on CVs targeted toward people in South America, Europe, and Asia.

Resources:

Resume tips for translators from Resume Writing for Freelancers by Beth Podrovitz and Jiri Stejskal.

"You need a CV that works," by Marta Stelmaszak.

Further actions

Once you have crafted a CV that you are happy with, you should also make sure that you protect it from those who would try to steal your information and use it in their own resumes. Sadly, CV fraud has become quite common these days among freelance translators. Because you have spent considerable time and effort polishing your resume, I highly encourage you to protect it from disingenuous translators who may try to steal your content and send it out to translation agencies as their own.

Here are some tips for protecting your CV:

- First of all, remove your CV from the Internet. Go to all the profiles you have online and remove it. You might even do a Google search for your resume to see where it is still online. Of course, there will still be cached versions for a while, but at least it's a start.
- When someone you trust requests to see a copy of your CV, create a password-protected PDF and send it to the potential client. Unfortunately, even a password-protected PDF can be opened with other non-Adobe versions of PDF readers. The safest alternative is to create an image file of your CV.
- Utilize your LinkedIn profile as an alternative (or complement to) your resume. Complete your profile with all the same descriptions, experience, and qualifications. Then, when a prospective employer requests to see your resume, simply ask them to connect with you there so they can have a look.
- Get your own domain name, and stop using Hotmail and Gmail. Then you can publish a

statement on your website that if someone is sending something, claiming to be you, but he or she is using a free email account, it is a fake.

Recipe 6: *Cover Letter*

A resume/CV is usually accom-panied by a cover letter, which is a one-page intro-duction to the resume that follows. So, the question becomes: Do freelance translators really need to worry about cover letters? Cover letters are usually written when translators apply for a permanent, full-time job. In the case of freelance projects, or short-term contracts, it is more common to simply include a proposal letter or letter with an offer of services.

Translation companies use the term "cover letter" as in "please send us a cover letter with your CV", but there's nothing wrong in educating them that in fact these are business proposals. Let's keep the new wording in mind throughout the process of creating such a letter. Remember that we offer services and we are not enquiring about jobs. This distinction will change your mindset and how you perceive your business.

If you are applying to an agency or company directly via e-mail however, you should include a proper cover letter. It should be concise, but it should resemble more an actual letter you'd send via snail mail than an elevator speech. The difference is that rather than attaching the letter in a PDF format, simply write it in the body of the email.

Follow this recipe for creating a compelling business proposal (cover letter) that wins you clients:

Ingredients

- Relevant information on the company you are contacting
- Contact person
- Resume

Steps

Keep in mind that prospective clients and employers are looking for evidence that you are the right person to fulfill their needs. Therefore, you should tailor your proposal in a way that demonstrates that you are aware of who they are and what they are looking for (this will require some research). Only then can you convincingly express that you are the right person for the job.

This process, however, of researching and rewriting can take valuable time – and it is time that you are not getting paid for. So how can we streamline the process? Chances are that you will notice that you are pretty much writing the same "speech" in every business proposal. Here are my tips for speeding up the process while still making each cover letter seem as though it were custom-made for each client:

1. **Know who you are writing to.**
   Even minimal research is better than no research at all. Know who your client is, what his/her company does, and express your knowledge of the industry.

2. **Know what you want to achieve with your message.**
   Write with a purpose and have a clear goal outcome in mind.

3. **Dispel their fears.**

   You may write: "I have completed over 100 projects to do with medical devices and have references from three of my regular clients." Or, "If you doubt my technology skills, I have been using InDesign for over two years and completed a training course at my university."

4. **Ask them to take action.**

   Help close the deal by including a call to action at the bottom. Perhaps you invite the client to meet you in person, or to give you a call to further discuss the project.

5. **Leverage the power of references.**

   Offer to make references and referrals available to the client upon request. Or even better, point them to your LinkedIn profile or website where you have referrals and testimonials.

6. **Follow up.**

   Politely conduct a follow-up via email or telephone within a week of your initial application. Ask if you can provide any additional materials that would assist in making their decision, or if you can clarify questions regarding your application. Keep it friendly and don't nag.

Steps to avoid

- **Addressing the letter with "Dear Sir/Madam," or "To whom it may concern."**
Unsolicited applications may work, but usually, they have a much lower success rate. Simply do a little research into the company and use the name of the contact person listed on the job listing or website.

Clients and recruiters don't want to waste their time reading applications from translators who are poorly informed or entirely wrong for the position. For example, I receive numerous applications addressed to Dear Sir/ Madam, from translators who work in a variety of language combinations. What's wrong with that? For one thing, had the applicant taken the time to visit my website or read any of my online profiles, he/she would be able to address the letter with my name and (more importantly) would know that I only work with two languages.

Professionals are expected to read and understand requirements in job offers, and shall definitely be able to do some research. Take your time to read ads and job offers thoroughly, do your homework by visiting the prospect's website, and find out who will receive your application or bid. Whenever possible, your marketing communication shall be addressed to a person rather than a company or a vague entity.

- **Including typos and poor grammar.**
If you are applying for freelance translation jobs it is imperative that all communication is written with impeccable grammar. Everything you present to a potential client is being used to evaluate your skills, qualifications and professionalism. You can't possibly expect someone to believe that you are a meticulous proofreader and careful translator if you submit a cover letter riddled with spelling errors and erroneous punctuation. Proofread multiple times, spell check everything, and have a second person edit your work whenever possible.

- **Not including information you were specifically asked to provide.**

  After you have written your cover letter, go back to the job offer/enquiry or website and double-check that you have included absolutely all the requested information. Professionals are expected to be able to carefully follow instructions. If you fail to do this in your cover letter, chances are the potential client is going to have a hard time trusting your reliability in the future. Once again, keep in mind that every interaction with the client and every piece of information you provide (or leave out) counts towards or against your chances of getting hired. Nothing you do is ever off the record.

- **Making the cover letter too long.**

  Particularly when it comes to projects that you are passionate about, it can be difficult to limit just how much you say in the cover letter. However, you have to keep in mind that your reader has very limited time and a short attention span. Therefore, be efficient and summarize your skills, focus on the added value that you offer, and highlight the benefits of working with you over other translators on the market. The purpose of your cover letter is to briefly present who you are and what you can do. It is not an elaborate play-by-play of your career and it should not be a repetition of your resume. Instead, it should be a compelling introduction to your resume – one that gets them to open up the PDF. Remember, you only have a few seconds to win their attention. Use them wisely.

 Resources:
Creating a cover letter template for translation jobs, by Johanna Gonzales (www.translatorslife.wordpress.com).

Cover letter mistakes, by Alessandra Martelli (www.mtmtranslations.com).

Cover letter writing for translators – how to do it right, by Maja Źróbecka (http://www.mylingua.pl/).

Further actions - Cover letter template

In case writing a cover letter is new to you, or if you're having trouble paring yours down to the most important content, here is a basic cover letter template that will get you started:

Dear [*name of project manager or recruiter*],

I am a [*insert relevant language pair*] translator based in [*city, country*] and I would like to offer my services to your [*agency / company*].

My specializations include [*insert specialization, i.e. business*] translations; due to [*experience or training justifying specialization. A few examples:*]

[*Writing down the fields you want to translate in and your experience in those fields can help you clearly define what you can and what you can't do. Make these specifications sound good, but be truthful. Remember, listing a hobby as a specialization can be a risky choice. Being an enthusiast does not necessarily qualify you as a specialist or expert within a particular subject matter, so be sure not to oversell your expertise.*]

Please refer to my resume for further information. [*Prompt them to take action!*]

[*In the next paragraph, list your education and unique language skills (or your job as an engineer) or doctor before you decided to become a translator. Include anything that will make you stand out or define you as an expert.*]

Please let me know if I can provide you with any additional information.

Regards, [*Your name*]

Even if your business is conducted primarily online, you don't want to be caught without a business card on hand. Though some may advise you otherwise, I am a firm believer that networking opportunities tend to happen when you least expect them and you never know when you will stumble upon someone who could potentially benefit from your translation services.

Professionally printing a small batch of business cards is one of the most cost-effective and widely used marketing tools in your pantry. It may be the only form of print advertising you ever invest in, and it may also be the most beneficial. Business cards are small, easy to carry, and easy to distribute. It also helps lend credibility to your online business so that when people ask you what you do, you can share your business card and receive a new business contact in return.

Ingredients

- Use a business card-creating program, either on your computer or through any of the business card services online, such as www.vistaprint.com, or www.moo.com. However, I do not recommend using the free versions. Freebie business cards generally print the design company's name on the back of the card and do not look professional. Instead, pay the small fee and make sure your brand is the only thing you are promoting.

- A professional printer. I do not recommend printing or cutting your own business cards at home. For a very affordable price you can go to a local printer and get them professionally prepared. Unfortunately, homemade business cards are usually easy to spot and don't benefit your business' reputation.

Steps

1. Make sure your name and all contact information is included on the card, is easy to read, and does not clutter the card with unnecessary information. Be sure to include your full name, email address, website, and telephone number (if applicable).

2. Include your language combination and your specializations.

3. Don't make it too specific, since this information might change frequently. You may decide to change your specializations at some point and do not want to be stuck with a stack of business cards that do not reflect your business. For that reason, I also recommend printing business cards in medium-sized batches.

4. Invest in an eye-catching logo. Having a standard logo that you can include online and in print will help establish your brand's identity. Though you may have to make a modest initial investment, in my experience it almost always pays off in the end.

5. Be generous. Printing business cards usually requires a very small investment, and you never know when they may be passed along to your next big client. Pass them out and don't hold back.

Resources:
Vistaprint (www.vistaprint.com), Moo (www.moo.com)

Chapter 4

Magnetic Marketing Tools

Now it is time to introduce some marketing tools that you use to attract clients, making them find you, instead of the other way around. That is why I call them magnetic. These tools will help you make potential clients more aware of you and the services you provide. With these tools you can also inform and educate them, creating a relationship that can make them know, like and trust you. One of my favorite tools for this is a website, which should be the hub for all your marketing efforts. It's the place you want potential clients or current clients to go for more information or to take action.

Recipe 8: *Your website*

A website is one of the best ways to maximize your online marketing and presence. When we want to

find something these days, what do we do? We Google it! Make sure your potential clients can easily find information about your professional translation services by having an optimized website and a strong online presence.

Your website is also your hub for all other marketing activities, a place where you can direct prospects to find out more about your translation services. When someone performs a search for your services, a website can "prove your existence" as a freelancer. As soon as the customer visits your website, he or she is convinced of the consistency and seriousness of your services.

These days you do not have to know HTML or hire a designer either to create a website. There are several services out there that make it really easy to create a website.

Here are some examples of web design and hosting services with easy templates for websites:

1. Blogger (www.blogger.com)
2. WordPress (www.wordpress.com)
3. Webs (www.webs.com)
4. Squarespace (www.squarespace.com)

There are many more, but these are the services I have personally used and I can guarantee that they are easy to use and reliable. The first three are actually blog platforms, but they work great for creating websites, too. The last service, Squarespace is geared toward artistic people, but works well for marketing translation services, too.

Ingredients

There are no absolute rules for what information your website should contain, but the following are suggestions for basic layout and how you want your website to look, and what basic information it should contain.

Home page

The home page is the landing page. This is where prospects come first, and it is here that you need to convince people to read further. Present your services in a compelling way, focusing on the value you can provide your clients and how your services are unique. When first creating a website, this can be the only page you have.

About page

On the about page, you should tell the visitor who you are, what your company does and preferably a story of why you are providing the services you do. Remember to not focus so much on you, but rather on how you can help your potential clients based on who you are.

Services page

When you develop your website further you should create a separate page where you describe the services you offer in more detail. The services for a translator can be translation, proofreading, voiceover, interpreting, desktop publishing, and more. You can provide examples of the projects you have done, what your specializations are and (if you have approval from your current customers) who you have worked for before.

Contact page

In order to make it really easy for potential clients to contact you, you should preferably have contact information on every page of your website. But it is also important to have a separate contact page, where you can provide all your contact information, and perhaps a form that the client can use to contact you and attach a document.

A page with sample translations and testimonials

Once a potential client is interested in your services, it is good to provide proof of your abilities. This can be done with testimonials from happy clients and sample translations so that the potential client can see your translation style and quality. These can be listed on a separate page.

Page with events, training, certifications, publications.

When you develop your website further, you can add a page where you list your education, degrees, courses and qualifications. If you have any certifications or publications, you can also list them here. These increase your credibility and expertise.

Multilingual

Since we are working as translators, it is a great idea to provide your website in all languages you work in. This can easily be done by linking between two identical sites, or using language plug-ins in Wordpress.

Steps

If you do not have a website, I recommend following these steps to create one for your translation business.

1.   Plan your website

Define what the purpose of your website is. This gives you focus when you develop the copy, layout and images for the site. For example, my online marketing brochure allows people to read more about me and my services. And thanks to SEO, I do not have to go out and search for many clients; they find me.

Think about how people will benefit from visiting your website. Will they learn more about your services, more about translation, see if you are what they are looking for?

Plan the content. What will your website contain? What pages, functions and such?

Think about what keywords you need to focus on to attract the most people. Keywords are used for search engine optimization, so that your site can show up higher in search results. They should describe your services. Do not be afraid to be more exact, and use longer keywords (several words) as long as it is something your potential clients might be looking for when searching for the services you provide. For me, some keywords would be: *Swedish translation services, Swedish software translation*, and *translate website into Swedish*, for example.

2.   Register a domain name

Register your own domain name from the start. It looks more professional than having someone else's brand name in the web address. This is not expensive. It can be as little as $8.95/year. Here are some examples of where you can register a domain name: http://www.GoDaddy.com or through the free hosting website. The domain name should be easy to spell, say, and not be too long.

3.   Choose a web hosting service

A **web hosting service** is a type of Internet hosting service that allows individuals and organizations to make their website accessible via the World Wide Web. Web hosts are companies that provide space on a server owned or leased for use by clients, as well as providing Internet connectivity, typically in a data center. The web hosting service should be affordable, have a good reputation, be secure and well equipped. When you choose a web hosting service you should consider design options, minimum downtime and reliability. The web hosting services I mentioned in the beginning of this recipe can provide hosting services for you, but these provide you with less flexibility for development and design. However, a fully company-hosted service makes it really easy to set up a site; they take care of everything for you. If you choose the self-hosted option, you own the space for the website on a server, and you have more flexibility and more options, but you have to handle more of the steps yourself and "get your hands dirty" in web development. The web host I recommend for self-hosting is Bluehost.

4.   Choose a website template

A template is the easiest way to start and gives you superior web design quality. All the service providers mentioned above have plenty of free templates to choose from. You can also find templates that cost a little bit more and these provide more design options. I started out with free templates and they worked great. Now I have more demands for the design, and still want to be able to edit the content myself, so a paid template works better for me.

5.   Customize your template

Once you have chosen a host and a template, you can start putting in your own content in the template. Add copy, images and logos until you are happy with the pages. For many of the templates, you can also change the color theme of the template to fit your style and brand. Make it easy to read the content on your website. Present the content in short paragraphs, use headings and bullets to break up the text, and make it easy and quick to read. Don't forget to proofread all your copy or text. Make sure you have a call to action on your pages (for example, *contact me for more information,* or *click here to read more*). Put the call to action high up on the page (above the fold) so that the viewer will not have to scroll down to see it.

Don't clutter your menu bar with too many pages. Place the most important ones as main pages "root folder" and the rest as sub-pages under the main ones.

6.   Search Engine Optimization

Search engine optimization (SEO) helps rank your website so that it will be found high up in the search results, and this is an important step. But I do not recommend putting too much research into SEO. Gone are the days when you could stuff your site full of keywords or use link sharing to make your site rank higher. Google changes its algorithms constantly. But one trend is clear. Google's algorithms are becoming more intelligent, more like a human, and they reward sites that focus on providing visitors value.

<u>Here are some basic tips for optimizing your site for search engines:</u>

- Focus on providing value for people, your visitors, not search engines.
- For each page, use a concise but meaningful title tag, i.e. the title of the page
- Install a tool for SEO, where you can enter keywords, a title tag and description for each page. This is text that does not necessarily show on the page, but the search engines will find it "behind the scenes".
- Avoid a static website with old content. Go back regularly to update it with courses you have taken, or perhaps a blog where you can inform clients of vacations or new specializations.
- Make sure there are no broken links or missing images. You can, for example, use this tool to help: <u>www.brokenlinkcheck.com.</u>
- Put a title and description on all your images, preferably by using keywords. Images have become more important for Google, and by connecting them to keywords or descriptions, they will more easily be found.

7. Publish your website

Once you are satisfied with the content and the template, it is time to press the magic button called "publish". Make your creation, your marketing go live, and start using it as an important marketing tool.

Market your website

Once you have published the website, you have to make sure potential clients will find it, too. You cannot simply rely on Google or SEO.

Here are some tips on how to market your website online:

- Put a link to your website in your email signature.
- Include your web address when you post in newsgroups, forums, discussions and so on.
- Include the link in other Online profiles and directories.
- Put the link on your Facebook, Twitter, ProZ, ATA, LinkedIn, translation association and forum profiles
- Do some basic search engine optimization, such as registering your own domain name, submitting the URL to the most common

search engines, and focus on keywords in headings and page titles.

How you can market the website offline:

Include your URL in all marketing communications:

- Business cards
- Resumes
- Brochures
- Christmas cards

 Resources:

Creating and optimizing a website for your freelance translation business – On-demand presentation at ProZ.com

Further actions:

Here are some more SEO tips if you want to dig a little deeper.

Search engines look at the following three main aspects of a website:

- Content quality
- Correct code
- Site indexing speed

- Sites that are slow to load are penalized in rankings. To make your site load faster, you can try to compress images without decreasing their quality too much. Another tip: avoid adding too many sidebar widgets and scripts (too many functions in the sidebars). To check how quickly your website loads, you can try using the "Pagespeed" app (http://tools.pingdom.com/fpt/). There are many other tools available for monitoring of site indexing speed

- Check for broken links with (for example) brokenlinkcheck.com

- Enable caching features for your website. These are usually tools that you can add to the functions of the site (such as Wordpress plugins).

Multilingual websites and SEO

- Do not confuse search engines with languages. Use separate subdomains or sub-folders for separate languages. Subdomains act as separate sites.

Google Analytics

In order to figure out who your visitors are and how successful your website is in attracting your ideal clients, you can use Google Analytics. Google Analytics is a service offered by Google that generates detailed statistics about a website's traffic and traffic sources and measures conversions and sales. It's the most widely used website statistics service. Google Analytics can track visitors from all referring sites, including search engines and social networks, direct visits and referring sites. It also tracks display advertising, pay-per-click networks, email marketing and digital collateral (such as links within PDF documents).

Chapter 5

Magnetic Marketing Tools: Social Media, Referrals, Testimonials and Publicity

Social media marketing is perhaps this decade's most beloved buzzphrase. For good reason too – social media is a term that encapsulates many different marketing tools.

So, the million-dollar question becomes: as a freelance translator, do I have to use social media?

Quite frankly, social media marketing can either be a phenomenal waste of time or it can be an excellent source of contacts and insights, depending on how you use it. I see social media as a great tool for freelance translators to connect with colleagues and potential clients, and it is totally free. All it requires is time.

Social networks offer a variety of business benefits. Social media can:

- Give you direct access to decision makers in your target industries
- Increase your exposure and build your online reputation as an expert

- Improve your visibility and SEO
- Give you an opportunity to expand into new business areas
- Help you network with colleagues and clients all over the world
- Stay informed about industry news and trends

As with all the marketing tools I present in this cookbook, the ones you use will depend on your business goals. It is certainly not necessary to be active on social media. Some translators do perfectly well without it, while others rely heavily on it to supply client leads and build a powerful online presence.

Don't feel that you have to dive into social media and create 50 profiles overnight. In the game of social networks, strategy wins out every time. Take a moment early on to determine what you hope to gain from using social media. By establishing a clear goal from the very beginning, you will be able to identify the tools and actions that will help you achieve your aims. Are you hoping to find new client leads, and if so, what kind of clients would you most like to work with? Are you hoping to build relationships with other translators who you can collaborate with, and if so, who are they? Or, would you just like an efficient way to share and gather information online?

Once you have identified and clarified what you would like to get out of social media, every subsequent action becomes much easier to take. Knowing your ideal outcome will help you identify which platforms to use, what content to post, who to connect with, and how to measure your impact.

Before we dive in to the social media tools that are most useful for freelance translators, I'll cover some general dos and don'ts for using social media in your business.

Do:

- Share, participate and be proactive.
- Have realistic expectations (Social media is not about instant gratification; it may take several months for the benefits to become evident.)
- Limit activity to no more than 2-3 networks.
- Protect your privacy by not sharing too much personal information (not related to your business).
- Proofread and edit all content before posting.
- Choose appropriate and different content for each network.

Social Media Don'ts:

- Don't just become a salesperson, or passively wait for clients to come to you.
- Don't dilute your attention across too many networks, you'll overwhelm yourself and poorly represent your business.
- Don't mix your personal and professional life.
- Don't share your political or religious views
- Don't repeat all posts across multiple networks (This is laziness, and your followers will have no reason to interact with you across networks).

There are literally thousands of social media networks available for business owners to choose from, so it's no wonder that many entrepreneurs find the options overwhelming. In this recipe I am only going to focus on the most delicious (and effective) ingredients for freelance translators. Though the most popular social media tools vary greatly from country to country, I recommend looking into the following networks and considering how they can be useful for your business:

LinkedIn

This business-oriented social network is a powerful resource for connecting with other businesses, translators, and for recruiting new hires.

Twitter

In 140 characters or less, Twitter allows you to upload timely news and updates to followers in your network.

Facebook

Perhaps the world's most popular social network, Facebook allows a forum for multimedia, long-form postings. On Facebook you can have both a personal profile and a business page.

Google+

Google's social network is steadily gaining ground

and allows you to connect with clients as they search online, all the while boosting your SEO.

Recipe 9: *LinkedIn*

In my experience, I have found LinkedIn to be the most important social media tool for freelance translators looking to boost their business. Therefore, if you feel like you can only manage taking on one social network, LinkedIn is the perfect place to begin. I mentioned earlier that LinkedIn can serve as an online version of your resume, but it can do so much more than that. Hundreds of jobs and networking opportunities are available on LinkedIn every single day, many of which are available entirely free of charge.

Colleagues and employers can add testimonials and public recommendations. These endorsements help communicate to potential clients that you are a reliable, trustworthy, and professional. You can also integrate your LinkedIn profile with the rest of your online identity by including links to your website, other social media profiles, articles you've written, seminars or presentations, whatever best applies. LinkedIn also allows you to link your account to your blog, meaning that new posts will be automatically displayed on your profile page. If you are affiliated with an important translation institution, such as ATA or Translators Without Borders, display their icons in your profile. This will show that you are active in the translation world and it will increase your online reputation.

By creating a free professional profile, you will join hundreds of companies and individuals in the industry who are all looking to promote themselves or to hire other professionals. In joining this platform you can have access to other translators in your area, job listings, news, and a variety of other industry information that can help you stand out in your field.

One of the advantages of LinkedIn is that your profile functions in a similar way to a website domain, meaning that all the information you post on LinkedIn has the potential to show up in online search results. Therefore, by publishing content that is targeted toward a specific niche, and by incorporating relevant keywords, you can take advantage of the SEO (Search Engine Optimization) benefits that LinkedIn offers. Unlike activity on other social networks, LinkedIn makes you visible not only to other LinkedIn members, but to anyone on the Web. That means big potential for positioning your business as a leader in your industry.

What are the most useful LinkedIn features?

LinkedIn is ideal for freelancers because it is geared towards connecting people with companies, recruiters with candidates, and freelancers with potential clients. Here is a brief overview of LinkedIn's most valuable features for your translation business:

- LinkedIn acts like a sort of continuous resume or CV, so professionals are able to search for people with the skills they need. For that reason, keeping your LinkedIn profile up-to-date is critical. You want to make sure that anyone who stops by to see your resume is seeing the most accurate summary of your skills and qualifications.
- You can reconnect with past clients to stay up-to-date with what they're working on and remain at the forefront of their minds, in case a new translation project arises.

- Past clients can 'recommend' you and endorse your skills, which is a powerful promotion tool.
- You can participate in discussions to help people looking for answers, or ask questions of your own. By doing so, you position yourself as a knowledgeable expert in the field, and gain visibility for your business. This is easiest done in groups in your subject area or in your field.
- LinkedIn has a job search function, although it's mainly used for permanent or long-term contract work, rather than consulting or freelance. However, it can be useful to see what companies are currently recruiting.

How do companies and recruiters use LinkedIn?

In many ways, LinkedIn is a dream tool for those that work in human resources. Rather than having to sift through stacks of paper resumes, recruiters are able to type in a few choice keywords, and easily browse through a variety of candidates online. Because LinkedIn is essentially an online database of CVs, available around the clock to people all over the world, finding a qualified professional has never been easier.

Traditional job searches on LinkedIn tend to be geared towards permanent or full-time positions. That is because companies have to pay a (sometimes considerable) fee to publish job vacancies within the LinkedIn database. In the case of freelance translation work, you may want to search for long-term contracts, or project-based work. It is not uncommon for recruiters to use LinkedIn as a tool to find contractors on behalf of their clients. In order to be visible in their searches, be sure to thoroughly complete your profile, company page, and optimize all headlines with powerful keywords.

Ingredients

- Basic profile information, including profile picture
- Good headline
- Summary
- Experience
- Education, courses, awards
- Connections with former and current colleagues and other people you know
- Recommendations
- Groups

1. **Sign up and create a professional profile.**
A basic LinkedIn account is free to create and use. You will be able to fill in your contact information, professional experience, education history, and a variety of other fields. Be sure to include a professional-looking profile picture (preferably a headshot with a friendly smile). Don't use your company logo in place of a portrait. People want to see you – the person behind the business! Use your headline and profile summary to briefly describe what you do. Be sure to include strong keywords such as 'English into Swedish translator' or 'French medical translator'. Remember to fill out as many of the available profile fields as possible, including links to your website or blog. The more complete your profile, the more likely you are to be perceived as an expert. Proofread your work thoroughly and click to publish!

2. **Connect with people you know.**
LinkedIn offers the option to import your contacts directly from Gmail, Hotmail, or Yahoo. However, I recommend separating your

business contacts from your personal contacts, and use LinkedIn exclusively for business networking. By keeping my LinkedIn profile purely work-related, I don't need to worry about my friends and relatives receiving my translation updates. Start by finding all your ex-colleagues and sending them requests to add them as a LinkedIn connection. Then, simply add new business contacts as you meet them, even if you just met them via a pitch or an interview. Quickly reaching out to new acquaintances on LinkedIn shows you're on top of things, interested in the person, and (in the case of job interviews) available for future work opportunities. Even if you don't get a job offer, connecting with your interviewer online increases your chances of securing a future position within the organization.

3. **Ask for recommendations.**
The best thing about LinkedIn is that people can publish endorsements about you and your work, which is a great way to demonstrate your worth to prospective clients. Though it may feel awkward at first, don't be afraid to request a recommendation from a past colleague or client if you think you did a good job for that person.

Sometimes the client might not reply, in which case the important thing is to not take it personally. Chances are that they simply have too many things on their plate. Don't let that stop you from asking other people. However, I do not recommend sending the standard recommendation-request message in an effort to prompt responses. Take a moment to edit the message and make it personal to the work you did. You may even mention that as a freelancer, you rely on positive testimonials in order to grow your business. Also mention how much you enjoyed working with the client and that you would be happy to provide a positive recommendation in return for the client's time. If you do wind up giving a reciprocal recommendation, it's a good idea to wait for a period of time so that people do not suspect you're in a mutual appreciation society with your clients.

4. **Create a company page (optional).**

Now that you've created a solid profile page for yourself, you can start using LinkedIn's more advanced features. That involves setting up a company page for your freelance business. This page is similar to a personal profile page, but it offers you the chance to display your logo, explain your services, and provide details regarding your past work. I also recommend integrating your company page with your Twitter updates and blog posts, as well as inviting your followers from other platforms to follow your LinkedIn company page. Chances are you won't need to invest too much time in your company page; it's more of a one-time set up. The main purpose of this page is to provide more information when people click on your job title, and to give credibility and authority to your business as a whole.

5. **Post status updates.**

   Much like Twitter and Facebook, LinkedIn allows you to update your personal profile with status updates. These updates appear on the homepage feeds of the people who are connected to you. As always, keep your posts work-related and professional. However, that isn't to say that you have to be salesy or stuffy. It's still perfectly respectable to have a personality, just don't sacrifice credibility for creativity. Be yourself and add links to interesting articles that are relevant to your audience, projects you're working on (as long as they're not confidential), or repost updates from your connections if you think the extra publicity would help them.

Add projects to your profile.

LinkedIn is constantly incorporating new features, one of which is a section that allows you to add details about projects that you are working on. This section is a powerful tool for freelancers who find themselves working with lots of different companies, but can't easily reflect this in the employment history section of the profile page. Add a few brief details about the project, the company, and any new skills, software, or notable obstacles or successes you encounter along the way. I also recommend adding the name of someone you collaborated with on the project, particularly if the client is senior in the organization. That person's contacts will then become aware of you and your capabilities, and your network will slowly but surely expand to incorporate new potential clients.

6. **Join some professional groups and follow some companies.**

   Associating with related professional organizations allows you to demonstrate your interest in the industry and keep up-to-date with developments and trends. Find companies you've worked for or would like to work for, or simply connect with companies you suspect may need a translator with your qualifications. Follow them to see their status updates, and reach out if you think they may be able to benefit from your services.

7. **Look at available jobs and see if you can get an introduction.**

   Use the job search function on LinkedIn to search for translation jobs. Although most jobs posted on LinkedIn are permanent or long-term contracts, you can get a sense of what companies are in the market for translation services. Perusing job offerings can also help you identify new businesses in your industry, or those undergoing lots of staff changes. It is always appropriate to write a polite letter or email to someone in the business, offering your CV in case something suitable comes up.

When you find a company that is looking for translators, you can follow that company's profile page and take a look at the 'employees' section. If you already have a direct connection to someone on the inside, that's great! If the company is a second-degree connection, you can then look to see who's a mutual connection and see if that person will introduce you. You may email the documentation manager or global marketing director to offer your services should either need help with a project in the future. Making companies aware that you are available to help is an excellent way to promote your services and it's even more effective if you can add a testimonial from your mutual contact.

8. **Try LinkedIn advertising (optional).**

You can pay to place short text ads on LinkedIn, which is cheaper than posting a job vacancy. You specify what sort of job function or job title you want to advertise to, the location, your daily budget for the advert and so on. Then anyone who fits your criteria will see your ad on their LinkedIn pages as they browse. Most will automatically ignore it, but it's often a very low-cost way to get a bit more exposure. I recommend you keep it running for a few months and use the in-built analytics to see how many times it was clicked. That will give you a better idea of whether the ad is worth continuing. If you notice an ad is not very effective, consider changing the design and copy, and running a new version to see if that better resonates with your target audience. You might get a job out of it, or you might be put onto someone's shortlist of emergency contractors they can call on in the future.

9. **Integrate LinkedIn with your website.**

   Your website should contain a link to your LinkedIn personal profile, as this is a good way to show off your connections, your industry expertise and experience. Don't underestimate a potential client's need for speed and an easy life. Your job is to overcome their doubts and reassure them that you are the best candidate to fulfill their needs. Demonstrate that you've worked for other companies in the market and that you have experience with similar processes and systems. If they don't need to provide too much training, you can get started quickly, and they're more likely to contact you.

10. Participate in your groups

Finally, to really increase your exposure, I recommend joining discussions or posting questions of your own in your LinkedIn groups. I've done this, and the number of people from the groups that view my profile after I've contributed to a discussion is surprising. They may not always be my target client, but I have received consulting requests as a direct result of Q&A sessions or posting a useful link to a group.

 **Resources**

Little Book of Social Media for Translators, by Nicole Y. Adams.

The Power Formula for LinkedIn Success by Wayne Breitbarth.

Episode 004: Using LinkedIn to market translation services – Interview with Anne Diamantidis (www.marketingtipsfortranslators.com).

Further actions

Here is an example of what you can do on LinkedIn in only 6 minutes a day:

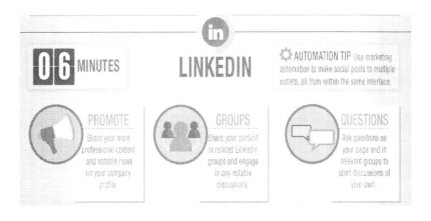

Figure 1 Infographic sourced from pardot.com

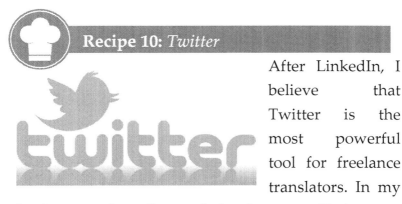

Recipe 10: *Twitter*

After LinkedIn, I believe that Twitter is the most powerful tool for freelance translators. In my business today, I regularly leverage Twitter to connect with potential clients, share content, and publish updates about my business. However – and I'm not ashamed to admit this – for a long time Twitter wasn't even on my radar, and I did not understand it. It wasn't until a colleague gave me a little nudge to get started that I began to better understand how I could promote my services on the platform. I began by creating my professional profile, connecting with a handful of colleagues and then slowly growing my network every day since. Now I am in love with it, so much so that I have to limit my daily Twitter time so I don't spend too much time on only one platform.

Unlike LinkedIn, Twitter is a real-time micro-blogging platform. What does that mean exactly? It means that users can publish small posts that are limited to no more than 140 characters and generally written in an informal tone. Whereas LinkedIn is almost exclusively geared toward professionals, Twitter has a much more social slant, and users post about absolutely any topic under the sun. Some people "tweet" (post) to connect with friends, while some use it to promote their business. In either case, Twitter is all about sharing timely comments and joining a global conversation, which absolutely anyone on Twitter can see. Twitter does offer the option to publish protected (semi-private) tweets, but mostly these are counterproductive for your professional marketing purposes.

Using Twitter as a marketing tool for your business offers a variety of different benefits. The sheer size of the Twitter network offers limitless networking possibilities, and the variety of content that you can publish offers an opportunity to position yourself as an expert within the industry. By being consistently active on Twitter, you will be able to boost traffic to your professional profile and your website. As is the case with LinkedIn, online search engines index everything that is published on Twitter. For that reason, it is important to optimize your profile and bio with powerful keywords.

Top 7 Twitter tips:

- Vary the types of tweets that you publish (including automated and personal tweets)
- Provide interesting links to others
- Post the most important messages multiple times at different times of the day (which will ensure that they are seen in different time zones)
- Participate in conversations (using hashtags)

- Acknowledge and support others (by retweeting or replying to their publications)
- Post consistently (I recommend posting daily)
- Include calls to action (For instance, posing questions and responding to your followers)

What you need to know to get started

Twitter comprises the immediacy of instant messages, the networking capacity of social networks, and the vast research potential of an Internet browser. On Twitter, short bits of information (140 characters per post) are shared immediately across a vast network of users. As is the case with all social media platforms, people are able to receive their messages on their computers and mobile devices in real time while at home, the office, or on the go.

Ingredients
- Twitter account
- Profile picture
- Background picture

Steps
At this point I hope you're beginning to feel inspired about using Twitter to promote your translation

services. However, it's one thing to have a personal Twitter account to socialize with friends, and it's an entirely different challenge to use it to market your business. Too many business owners forget to keep these two worlds separate, and the consequence is that they wind up damaging their business' reputation in the long run. If you want to make the best of Twitter for your professional career, here are some ideas to put into practice.

1. **Create your profile.**

   When you first create your profile, be sure to make it professional. If you already have a Twitter account for personal purposes, create another one for your professional presence. As always, don't forget to add a picture that appropriately represents your personality and professionalism (and it's not a bad idea to use the same picture across different platforms – it will help people quickly identify who you are). Include links to your website, blog, and other social networks. Twitter is also a great way to redirect people to your more detailed profiles and online CV (over at LinkedIn, for example). When you set up your account, you will have the option to import your contacts from your email account and other media. Again this is a personal call. I recommend only importing contacts that are relevant to your business. It's also important to keep in mind that the more followers you have, the more exposure your tweets will receive.

2. **Be authentic and social.**

Once your profile is complete, your challenge becomes following other people and getting people to follow you. Decide what translation institutions, language organizations, agencies, target companies and colleagues in your field you are interested in. Find their profiles on Twitter and start following them. You can also find companies and agencies in LinkedIn by using the advance search option. In this way, you will find interesting translation organizations or professionals in your fields and you can check if they use Twitter. It is a mutual etiquette to follow people who follow you, as a way of returning the favor, but it is not absolutely necessary. Likewise, it is a good strategy to follow people you want to be followed by.

Since Twitter makes it easy to get quick responses, agencies use it to keep in touch with translators and find candidates for some of their projects. For example, if they need a translator in a specific area or if they have an urgent translation, they can send a tweet to their followers, who will, in turn, retweet to their contacts.

Remember that Twitter is designed to socialize and is not designed for marketing. Marketing is an added value that comes from being active in the community by replying to other people's tweets, engaging in conversations that are already taking place, retweeting interesting content, commenting, posting useful information, and following other users. Think of Twitter as a place where people go to connect with other people they're interested in, a kind of happy hour setting. If you're new to the scene and want to make connections, don't burst in shouting, "I'm available! I'm a translator! Hire me!" The best thing to do is to decide which agencies and outsourcers you would most like to work for, and then you follow them, read and comment on their tweets, and little by little create an authentic relationship. Then, you can offer your services by saying that you like the style of an agency and you would like to be part of their team.

3. **Find, share, and learn.**

In the meantime, you can use Twitter as a platform to share your experience and knowledge, exchange information, interesting articles, and industry tips. To make the best of Twitter, you need to enjoy being "up-to-date" and well informed on topics related to the translation world. Find or create interesting content to share with others, which gives people a reason to tune into what you have to say. This information could be your own material (a link to your blog) or some other useful resources you found on the web. Both options are equally valid. If you find yourself stumped about what to share, simply ask yourself, "As a professional, what do I know that I can share?" You may find that you can talk about the latest trends in the industry, the recent CAT tools launched, and new workshops in medical terminology in your country or online, etc. Did you come across a great tutorial that really made it easier for you to learn a new tool? Tweet it!

4. **Don't be afraid to show your style and personality.**

Part of positioning yourself as an expert in the field, requires showing people a piece of what makes you unique. You can post the most fascinating articles in the world, but unless you have a personality, people are going to have trouble remembering who you are. Help your business stand out by building up your Twitter style. For instance, if you specialize in literature, you can regularly send a phrase by a known writer related to words, translation or life. As long as you stay professional, and never sacrifice quality for cleverness/ creativity, you'll be just fine.

5. **Ask questions and engage.**

In essence, Twitter can be seen as a worldwide public forum to exchange views an opinions. Ask questions on industry-related topics. Interact with others by answering questions and discussing a certain topic. This is a good way to learn about the experience of your colleagues, get a feel for the hot topics in your industry, and expand your professional network at the same time.

6. **Share your here and now.**

What's happening? What are you doing? Talk about your present situation. Don't be afraid to tell your followers about your current projects, tweet about the workshops or seminars you are attending. Tweet field-specific material. If you find a good glossary on a certain area, you can share it with your fellow translators. Soon enough, they will return the favor. In this way, Twitter may also become a tool to share useful resources that will facilitate your work. You'll find that a little professional transparency will help humanize your brand and will open you up to new opportunities and relationships with your clients.

 **Resources**

Social Networking and Translation: Twitter, by Julieta Spirito.

Twitter for translators, by Marta Stelmaszak (SlideShare).

How to find people on Twitter

Hashtags (#) are used as a kind of keyword, which organizes individual posts into conversations based on certain topics. You can use these hashtags in individual posts in order to target your publications and put them in front of users who are also talking about your industry. In the case of freelance translation, some popular hashtags include:

- #xl8 and #t9n (for translation)
- #xl8or (for translator)
- #l10n (for localization)
- #1nt (for interpreting)
- #i18n (for internationalization)
- #g11n (for globalization)
- #translation
- #language

Avoid this on Twitter:
- Being too professional or salesy rather than "human" and showing a personality
- Providing too much personal information
- Not engaging with other Twitter users
- Programming automatic direct messages (DMs)

- Retweeting only to self-promote
- Tweeting too frequently or too infrequently
- Overusing hashtags (limit yourself to no more than 2 per post)
- Using protected tweets

Some great tools to simplify your activities on Twitter:

- Tweetdeck
- Hootsuite

Here is a sample schedule showing how you can use Twitter in only 10 minutes a day.

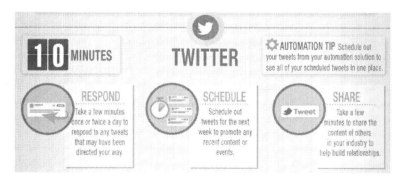

Figure 2 Infographic sourced from <u>pardot.com</u>

Facebook is arguably the world's favorite social media platform, and while thousands of new networks are cropping up every day around the world, Facebook has still remained the largest social network. I first began using Facebook for personal use, primarily to stay in touch with friends and family in far off places. However, in recent years Facebook has unleashed a massive marketing potential for businesses large and small. In fact, many businesses are able to exist with just a Facebook page and no external website whatsoever. While I don't recommend ditching your website by any means, it simply goes to show that the potential of Facebook as a marketing tool simply cannot be ignored.

As is the case with Twitter, Facebook can be used for both personal and professional purposes. However, the difference is that Facebook offers users two distinct profile options: a personal profile page or a company page. The personal profile is mainly for keeping in touch with friends and family and sharing news about your life, while the business page allows companies slightly different features and restrictions. Business pages can be managed by multiple people at once; they can create advertisements and paid promotions, communicate directly with customers and share specific information and news on topics including services, products, events, and achievements.

Ingredients

- Profile page with an image and/or company page
- Privacy settings (do not mix personal and business information)
- Lists of business contacts (allow them only limited access to your personal profile)
- Translation-specific Facebook groups such as:
  - Watercooler Network
  - ProZ.Com
  - Certified Pros Group
  - The League of Extraordinary Translators
- Professional organizations such as ATA and ITI
- Pages of interesting colleagues and agencies

- A custom URL (web address) to make your business page easier to find.

Steps

If you're interested in leveraging Facebook to market your freelance translation services, you'll need to create a Facebook Business Page, sometimes referred to as Fan Pages. These pages allow you to create and maintain a professional presence for your brand on Facebook. While you will want to create a business page for your brand, you can still use your personal page to funnel in contacts and earn engagement. This is particularly helpful because you'll probably find that many of your business contacts are also your friends. Keep in touch with them by keeping both profiles active. Just keep in mind that everything you do online is permanent and reflects on your business and brand.

1. **Create an attractive business page.**

   Think of your Facebook page as an online version of your translation storefront. This is where people come to window shop, to peek inside your business' front door and find out whom you are and what you are working on. For that reason, your page should be visually attractive, with images, pictures – not just logos and words. Encourage people to comment and "Like" your page. Keep your audience in mind; the tone of what you write or publish must be cheerful and relaxed – a tone that is appropriate for the social nature of Facebook.

2. Keep Your Timeline Updated.

By keeping your page (or "timeline") updated you will be able to show that your business is active and thriving. Post projects that you are currently working on, or mention services that you are offering at the moment. It's also a good idea to include translation courses, language seminars or interesting workshops you have attended recently. Doing so will demonstrate that you are constantly learning and improving yourself as a professional translator.

3. Take time to interact.

Of course there are a million things going on each day, but frankly there is no use setting up a Facebook page if you are not going to spend some time reading, searching for information on the web, answering your followers' questions, and interacting with your Facebook contacts. If you struggle to get this done, I recommend simply setting a daily goal. How many people you want to connect with? How much time you want to spend on Facebook?

4. **Become a source for great, multimedia content.** Beyond simply joining in on conversations happening on Facebook, you also want to give people a compelling reason to stop by and visit your business page. How do you make that happen? By becoming a known source for information that people care about. Sure, you'll only need to upload information that is relevant to your business and industry, but that doesn't mean it has to be stale content. Share pictures, videos, and images that you think your audience will find engaging. For example, you can upload pictures of the moment you received your translation degree at University or with your classmates at a Language Congress. You can also customize your page according to your field of expertise. If you specialize in tourism and travel, you may include some nice pictures of places to visit in your country.

5. **Interact with translation-focused groups and people.**

   Send invitations to connect with people related to your field, like pages of people of similar interest. Post updates or comments on translation and language groups, agencies or professionals involved in your fields of expertise. Join translation-centered groups and participate in the conversations that are taking place. You can even start forums on certain topics or ask questions to get them answered by professionals with experience. Like pages of associations like American Translators Association or Translators Without Borders, International Freelancers Academy or others related to specific kinds of translations. Slowly but surely, interacting with these groups and people will help build your reputation in the industry, while at the same time it will teach you about the trends and developments in your area of expertise.

6. **Integrate your Facebook page with other social media platforms.**

   Add links to your website, blog and other social media, including Twitter and LinkedIn. This way you can interact with contacts in these networks as well or redirect people to your other profiles.

7. **Stay proactive.**

   If you are offered a big translation project that you simply don't have the time to take on, post the job offering in a translation group. Chances are someone else will snap up the work in a heartbeat. You can also share resources with fellow translators, such as glossaries and vocabularies, particularly those that are designed for specific fields such as videogames, medicine, IT, technology, legal etc. You can even create an open glossary and encourage specialized translators to add words. The more you share, the more people will like your page and the more online presence you will gain.

The possibilities are endless. Your opportunities will depend on what you want (marketing, visibility, expanding your contacts, learning, or exchanging information) and the time you devote to updating your page and maintaining your contacts. You can choose some of the ideas I mentioned or you can use them as inspiration and come up with some of your own.

 **Resources**

Little book of Social Media for Translators, by Nicole Y. Adams.

The Freelance Translators' Guide to Using LinkedIn, by Louisa Stockley, whitepaper from SDL.

Facebook pages for translators (www.7brands.com).

Further actions

What not to do on Facebook:
- Write lengthy posts with far too much text
- Blatantly ask people for likes and shares
- Auto-publish from Twitter
- Forget to engage with your Facebook community
- Post too infrequently or not frequently enough

Here is an example of what you can do to keep up with Facebook in just six minutes a day.

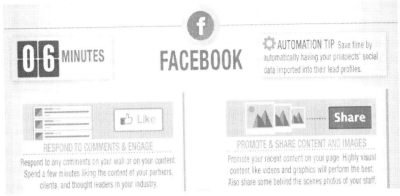

Figure 3 Infographic sourced from <u>pardot.com</u>

Google+ (Google Plus) is a relatively new social media platform and is starting to gain traction among translators and business professionals across a wide range of industries. Activity on Google+ brings many of the same rewards as other social media networks, with the added benefit of boosting your business' ratings in the meantime.

As you create and share content via Google+, your postings are shared with your "circles," or networking groups divided into categories of your choosing. You may decide to divide your audience into current clients, past clients, leads, coworkers, and friends and family. You have the capacity to target one group at a time or share content with several audiences at once.

Most businesses gravitate to Google+ because of the SEO benefits it brings to their businesses. The content you post on Google+ is visible in Google searches, and as a result builds up your online identity and status as an expert in your industry. There are also ways to link your blog to your Google+ account and cross-publish content in order to earn a wider readership.

Ingredients

- Google+ basic profile with profile picture and background picture
- Google+ page (optional)

Steps

1. Sign up and create a profile and connect with people in different "circles"

Circles are an essential part of Google+. They're the key to sharing. With Circles, people see all of the content that you want them to, and none of the content that you don't. You decide who can see each piece of personal information on your profile. For example, your contact details and relationship information could be visible to your friends' circle, while your employment history and education could be visible to your alumni association circle.

2. Put interesting information in your bio

3. **Link to all your other profiles and your website**
4. **Topics and content**

As with every social media platform, it's not about how many likes/ shares you collect, as much as it's about whether or not you are interacting with the right group of people. Search the Google+ database for relevant content, share it with your networks, and establish yourself as a thought leader.

5. **The "plus 1"**

Much like Facebook Likes, the Google Plus 1 is a way of calculating a particular post's popularity. The more +1's a post receives, the more visible it is to other users on the platform.

6. **Communities**

Google+ communities allow you to interact with niche groups related to a particular topic, such as translation or linguistics. Browse for topics related to your business and actively engage with members. You'll be able to stay up-to-date with their notifications and events in the meantime.

7. Pages

Google+ users are able to create personal profile pages as well as business pages that connect to company websites and boost a brand's presence. Posting to a business page allows you to post as the company itself, rather than having to use your personal name.

8. Tags, links and hashtags

Similar to Facebook and Twitter, you're able to tag contacts by using the @ symbol, which allows you to share your content directly with a person and his or her network. You can post links to outside content and tag posts with specific hashtags, as a strategy to organize your posts according to topic and conversation type.

Tools

Google+ offers many excellent tools and tactics to promote your business and build your brand's presence. Actively using these tools and posting relevant content frequently over an extended period of time can yield excellent marketing returns. Add your colleagues and clients, search out translation-related communities, and have fun promoting your brand!

Resources

A beginner's guide to Google+ for translators, by Sebastian Haselbeck (www.lingo.io).

Six Steps to Getting Started with Google+ - Social Media Examiner (www.socialmediaexaminer.com).

 Recipe 13: *Blogging*

In the past decade, blogs have exploded in popularity and have become more heavily trafficked than most forums and more effective than most email groups. Blogs allow people to self-publish content online (posts and articles) and they can also spur fantastic online conversations. A blog post can be the start of an open-

175

ended discussion, achieving a level of interaction that static web pages simply cannot. Readers can add comments to blog posts that critique the content, pose additional questions, or offer up additional information.

Businesses may decide to start a blog for any number of reasons – to network with colleagues, to position a brand as an expert, to foster community growth, etc. In this book, I am going to focus specifically on blogging as a marketing tool for translators to find and connect with prospective clients.

Blogs are an excellent networking tool for translators, since they offer an opportunity to join discussions among colleagues from all over the world. If you are not ready to start your own blog, you can still provide good value. Commenting on other people's blog posts is a great way to immerse yourself in the world of blogs. By commenting, you can offer useful information to other people who read the blog, without taking on the commitment of writing your own blog. You can also consider pitching a post idea to a blog that is related to your industry. Perhaps the blog's administrator would be interested in receiving a guest writer and giving you a bio box with a link back to your home website. These are great methods to test if you enjoy blogging before committing to having your own blog.

Should you start a blog?

The answer to that question is something you will have to determine for yourself. If you are interested in beginning a blog, I suggest moving forward if you can honestly make a commitment to publishing new, fresh, interesting content on a regular basis. Do not take on this project if you are likely to write three posts and then get bored and abandon the project.

It's also important to recognize that while it may be fun, blogging is also very time-consuming. Even if you don't blog on a regular basis, you have to find the time to actually write and edit your blog posts.

Because of the effort and time commitment involved in getting a blog launched, you'll need to be sure that you are making a worthwhile return on your investment. You may spend your precious time blogging rather than working and it may be difficult to determine what effect – if any – your blog is having on your business' bottom line. It's easier to measure the effectiveness of your website or your <u>direct mail campaign</u> than blogging efforts. I know many busy and successful translators who don't blog and yet they manage to find more clients than they can handle. Blogging is a tool in your marketing arsenal, but just like with social media, cannot directly be linked to a higher income or more clients.

How blogging can indirectly lead to more clients:

- You can build a professional network of colleagues and clients, who may later recommend your translation skills to people outside of your immediate network
- You can showcase your writing skills and demonstrate your expertise within a specific area
- You can improve your search engine ranking and overall brand visibility online
- For a low cost, you can occupy a larger space in your industry and "advertise" your services in a way that is not possible in other channels
- You can help potential clients by providing valuable information or tips about the translation buying process

If you consider starting a blog or if you already have a blog, make sure you have some well-defined goals for your blog and incorporate this method into your marketing plan, preferably with a content calendar.

Ingredients:

- Subjects to write about
- A website with blog functionality, or a blog space online
- Publishing plan/ content calendar
- Dedication, creativity, organization

Steps

Before starting your professional blog, you should consider the following:

1. What do you want to achieve with your blog? What business outcome would I most like to achieve through my blogging efforts? (Also, critically examine if a blog is truly the right vehicle to achieve this outcome.)

2. Who is your target audience? A blog written for other translators is not very likely to attract potential clients to your business. If you want to market your translation services, you are going to need to blog for your potential clients and speak directly to their needs.

3. What are you going to write about? I recommend creating a massive brainstorm list of potential ideas, getting every last one on

paper. Then you can go through and weed out the article topics that may not be appropriate for your blog. Once you are left with the strongest topics, create a blogging calendar about what articles you will publish and when.

4. Where should you host your blog? The best solution is to host your blog on your website. This is easy to do if you use WordPress or a similar content management system for your website. Hosting your blog internally will help increase the SEO for your website. If you do not have a website, you can start blogging on an external platform.

5. How are you going to let your target audience know about your blog? Think about where your potential readers hang out online and try to promote your blog there by commenting on their blog posts, by tweeting to them, or other non-intrusive ways of marketing. Also be sure to share all your blog posts across every one of your social media platforms.

Now that you have a better idea about what your blog is going to target and how it will be structured, it's time to turn up the intensity and target all of your blogging actions to help you attract more clients to your business. Here are my top tips for turning your blog into a client magnet:

6. Become crystal clear about who your target audience is. It may even be helpful to try to write directly to the person you imagine being your ideal client. This will help you have a focused idea about what clients' needs are and the tone/writing styles that will most resonate.

7. Write quality content. Some business bloggers are tempted to sacrifice quality for quantity of blog posts or for keyword-saturated content. Remember that your blog's central goal is to position you as a leader and expert in your industry and give potential clients a sample of your quality services. You will never be able to achieve that goal by publishing sub-quality content, no matter how high you rank in the search engine results.

8. Position yourself to help. Once you understand your target audience, you will also understand what that audience's most pressing needs are. Tap into that knowledge. Ask yourself, what do my clients need to know? What do they need help with? What frustrates them? How can I be of service? Use the answer to those questions as the subject for your articles. Write content that solves problems.

9. Share your expertise and success stories. Remember, you are the expert on your business and on your industry. Share stories about how your services helped clients succeed and in turn help potential clients get inspired about the possibilities you offer.

10. Be a source of information. Share conference reviews (conferences where your clients go) and presentations that potential clients are interested in. Become an aggregate of information that your clients finds useful and position your business as a leader and a valuable resource.

Resources

Episode 006: Blogging for Translators – Interview with Catherine Christaki from Lingua Greca. (www.marketingtipsfortranslators.com)

How to keep blogging for a really long time, by Corinne McKay (www.thoughtsontranslation.com).

The Case against Blogging, by Karen Tkaczyk (www.thoughtsontranslation.com).

Further action

If you decide to use blogging as a method of marketing your freelance translation services, it is best to create 5-10 blog posts in advance, before launching your blog. Having this small inventory of articles will help you not stress out about finding something to blog about every week, and you will be able to achieve a more relaxed approach to your writing.

Another great idea is to create a publishing schedule for your blog. This should only be an aid in keeping your posts coming regularly and will keep your focus on your target audience's needs and interests. However, don't let a schedule make you feel that you have to post something, even if you do not have anything to write about. High value content posted less regularly is much more valuable than content written just to get a post out according to schedule.

Recipe 14: *Networking*

The very idea of networking is often enough to make any business owner or professional more than a little nervous. However, it is also the most cost-effective and important way to reach out to clients, if done right. The goal of networking is to develop relationships (which might lead to business opportunities in the future). However, business outcomes should not be your main goal when first establishing contact with a new acquaintance. If you approach a stranger with the explicit goal of advancing your business, you are likely to come off as overly pushy and disingenuous. Instead, simply try to relax and be yourself. Approach every introduction as an opportunity to meet someone new – not as an opportunity to get ahead.

Purpose of networking

- Meet potential prospects
- Identify potential alliances
- Establish centers of influence
- Discover new vendors of needed products and services

Ingredients

- Online networking
- Networking in person
- Elevator speech
- Referrals and testimonials

Steps

1.   Networking online

The opportunities for networking online are so vast that they require their own recipe. Please see the sections on social media for more information on networking online.

2.   Networking offline

Networking in person is not as difficult as you may imagine. In fact, you likely are surrounded by a vast network of untapped resources and don't even know it. I recommend starting by reaching out to your local community, going to your chamber of commerce networking events, attending local business group trade fairs and the like. Think of it as a way to get new friends and contacts and the perfect excuse to get out of the house. Any business outcomes that result from your networking will come as an added benefit sometime down the road.

I also recommend that you come prepared with an elevator speech (that means a 2-3 sentence explanation of who you are, what you do, and who you can help). As you mingle at the event, focus on asking a lot of questions and being a good listener. Jot down a few facts about the person on the back of the business card. Organize the cards into categories such as: potential clients, referrer, vendor, general. If you have a smart phone, I recommend adding new contacts into your phone as soon as you get home. You can also save any details of your conversations into the 'notes' section of your contact page, that way you can be reminded of what you talked about the last time you spoke.

3.   Face-to-face networking and using an elevator speech

Live networking has time and time again been mentioned by fellow translators to be the number one way to attract new clients. There is nothing more effective than going to an industry event where your potential clients hang out, and talking to as many people as possible.

Networking novices often assume that meeting someone at a networking event is the prime time to give a sales pitch and to ask for business favors. That is entirely the wrong approach. The first meeting with a new contact is a time to get to know each other on a more personal level, in order to establish an authentic connection and friendship. Before launching into a speech about your business, ask yourself: Is this the appropriate time and place to have this conversation? Am I fully prepared and equipped with presentation materials? The answer is probably no.

With that in mind, why diminish your chances of making a favorable impression at networking events?

Always keep in mind the cardinal rule of networking: the first meeting is only an opportunity to make a favorable impression, not an opportunity to make a sales presentation. Utilize your 30-second elevator speech to introduce yourself and agree on a more appropriate time to discuss issues of mutual interest.

4.   **30-second elevator speech**
   - It is an interactive process – not a passive activity
   - Short presentation that draws a clear mental picture for other people
   - Create intrigue, and interest to learn more
   - The main goal is to make a favorable impression.

5.   **Networking events**

Here are some examples of networking events that translators can go to:
   - Professional associations (e.g. AUSIT, ATA, CIOL) > within your industry
   - Local Chamber of Commerce events > outside your industry
   - Business networks > within and outside your industry

6. Exchange business cards or contact information

One of the main goals for networking is to gain new contacts. You never know when a contact can help you or if you can help someone. Gather business cards and contact information at events in order to develop new business relations.

7. Follow up

Do not throw away your newly found possibilities with new contacts. Follow up after an event by connecting on social media, sending a thank you note or email and try to provide something useful for your new contact, such as a link to a resource or article.

 Resources

The Little Book of Networking for Translators, by Nicole Y. Adams.

Working the Room – Tips by Chris Durban (www.linguagreca.com/blog/)

Referrals and testimonials are among the most powerful marketing tools you can put to use for your translation services. Testimonials (written statements from customers) are a great marketing tool because they give past customers the opportunity to tell potential customers what they found most beneficial about you and your services. An endorsement from a third party gives you and your business the credibility you need to build a larger client base. In essence, they get a chance to do the marketing for you. Use testimonials in marketing by gathering praise from current customers and sharing that information in a variety of ways.

Ingredients

- Testimonials from happy clients
- Referrals from happy clients

How to gather testimonials for marketing purposes:

Ask for testimonials from your best clients. Your best clients should either be long-term customers, customers who have offered you repeat business, people that have already expressed appreciation for your work, or clients that you most enjoyed working for. I recommend contacting them and politely asking if they would be willing to provide you with a testimonial that you could feature in your marketing materials. You may suggest a letter, an email, or just a few comments describing your product or service and why they liked it. Make sure they know you will be using the testimonial for marketing and always ask for permission before you include your client's name or photos in any public place.

Thank people who compliment you. When you or your business gets a compliment, ask the person raving about you to put it in writing. Then thank them for their kindness!

How to Market with Testimonials

If you are holding onto positive testimonials and feedback, leveraging that information can do wonders for your marketing strategy. However, in order to make the most of them, you'll need to use a few simple strategies that will guide you to get the most out of every word.

Feature testimonials on your company website and social media platforms.

Prospective clients are perusing your website to learn more about your company and the quality of your services. By providing a few compelling testimonials you can help lower the risk that potential clients face when deciding to hire you. Demonstrate to them that you are capable, that you have ample work experience, and that past clients are pleased with your services. I recommend dedicating a page (or specific section) for testimonials. Update the testimonials regularly, or rotate them in and out so that if clients circle back around they are provided with new reviews. It can also be extremely helpful to invite people to submit reviews directly via your website or social media profiles.

Include testimonials (or testimonial excerpts) on your marketing materials, whether they are in print or produced digitally. This may include flyers, brochures, postcards, and paid advertising.

Bring stories up in conversations! If you have a client success story or are holding onto a raving review, bring it up in conversations with potential clients. Whether you're having a casual conversation, or delivering a sales pitch, present your translation services with confidence and don't be shy about sharing a few words of praise that clients have shared with you. Just be sure not to overdo it.

Referrals

In my experience, referrals (or word-of-mouth references from clients or colleagues) are one of the most effective ways to grow your business and incorporate new clients. When you provide a high quality service and successfully establish positive relationships with your clients, chances are that they will later become your brand advocates. Past clients that advocate for your brand are those that defend your services, sing your praises, and put you in touch with other people that can benefit from what you do.

Many new translators struggle to get more referrals, but in my experience the most effective strategy is simply to ask for them.

Some translators assume that a satisfied customer will voluntarily submit a testimonial, while others are too shy and nervous to even contemplate requesting one. Letting a happy client walk out the door is one of the biggest mistakes you can make, and doing so means that your business has to start from scratch every time you need a new influx of clients.

How to Get Over Your Fear of Asking for Referrals

I do understand that the squeamishness can be a big hurdle for some people to get over. It does sometimes feel uncomfortable, but that does not mean that you have an excuse to chicken out. Here are some of my favorite tips for building up the courage to ask for referrals:

- Remember that most people like to help other people (particularly when the good

deed comes at no personal cost, as is the case with referrals)
Remind yourself that the worst that can happen is that the client says, "No." And if that were to happen, simply smile, and thank them for their business.

- Make asking for a referral part of your project routine. With most projects, there's a last meeting with the client. This final meeting is the perfect time to ask for a referral. By incorporating this simple question into your routine, you'll get in the habit of collecting referrals at the end of every translation project you complete.

 Resources
How to ask for referrals and get more clients, by Susan Ward (sbinfocanada.about.com).

Further actions
Scripts for asking for a referral

In case your fear is really powerful, I recommend having a simple script in mind that you can fall back on any time you find yourself tongue-tied. It's also important to remember that you're not making an Oscar acceptance speech here. When you ask for a referral, be sincere and direct. You may decide to say something along the lines of:

"I'm really glad that you're pleased with my work. I'd really appreciate it if you'd pass my name along to anyone else you know who would be interested in _____ (what you do).

Leaving extra business cards with a person makes it easier for them to pass your name and contact information to someone else. Another variation of this script is to be even more direct and ask for names when you're asking for referrals. For instance, you might say:

"I'm really glad that you're pleased with my work. I'm always looking for referrals and wonder if you know anyone else who might be interested in _____ (what you do)."

Pause here and see what the client says. Some people will offer some names. Some will say, "Yes, maybe," and not offer any further information. Some will say, "No," but at least you tried.

If clients do offer names, take them down and ask if they would mind if you contact the people directly, or if they would prefer to pass your information along themselves. If they don't offer names, ask if you can leave some additional business cards with them that they can pass them along.

Recipe 16: *Publicity*

To get the word out about your business and your expertise, you can use publicity and public relations to help gain positioning within the marketplace. Publicity is something someone else writes or says about you and your company when you do something noteworthy and interesting. There are many business benefits from good publicity, but the most important is that it is much more effective than advertising when it comes to visibility. You can help spread the word by creating your own press releases. Even with the increasing popularity of blogs and online content, press releases are still a tool in the marketing arsenal that you can use to reach your ideal clients.

To summarize, here is what PR can do for your freelance translation business:

- Bring traffic to your website
- Get people talking about you and your business
- Position you as an expert within your industry
- Boost awareness of your brand
- Establish your credibility
- Make potential clients aware of you

Ingredients

- Press releases
- Articles
- Public speaking

1. **Create a press release**

   A press release consists of five parts:

   - Headline: To grab attention and introduce the primary subject matter
   - Sub-headline: Short, compelling introduction to the content, which contains more context and clarifying details than the headline
   - Lead paragraph: Contains the major facts of the story and responds to the questions who, what, where, when, and why
   - Remaining paragraphs: Develops the story in greater detail
   - End: Provides pertinent information about the business and the owner

Here is an example of the standard press release layout and the content that it should contain:

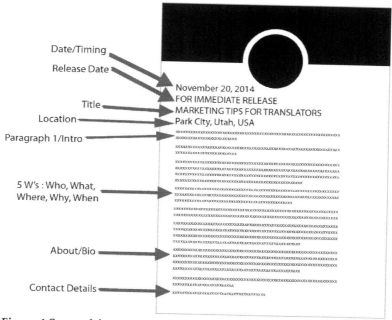

Figure 4 Sourced from: www.buildawebsitetonight.com

When you are finished with the press release you can submit it to local newspapers and to online public relations (PR) submission sites such as freepressrelease.com and others.

While the press release may be the most traditional way to generate publicity for your translation company and translation services, there is a wide range of other options to choose from. Here are some additional actions you can take to earn positive PR for your business:

2. Article writing

Article writing is a great way to spread the word about your expertise in a specific subject. Pick a subject that your target audience is interested in and that you know a lot about. You may have to do some additional research in order to round out the content, but as long as you are confident that everything in the article is as accurate as possible, you should be in the clear.

As you write your article, be sure that you include a compelling title, one that puts a unique spin on the content you present and is likely to entice readers to take pause. The article should be logically structured to include an introduction, development section, and conclusion. You may decide to present a problem, explain what the situation looks like before the problem has been solved and illustrate how the situation changed after the problem has been solved. You may offer a how-to article with some of your top tips. Or you may tell a story, present a problem, and propose a solution. However you decide to structure your article, be sure that it is engaging and that it includes a call to action at the end.

When you are happy with your article, and have thoroughly proofread it to eliminate any grammatical errors, you can submit it to publications read by your target market. For example, you may decide to submit it to the ATA Chronicle, industry magazines, or to article databases. You should also post the article on your blog or website and cross promote in on your social media platforms. Your goal is to write powerful content that your target audience will want to read, share, and engage with. I've also found that a great tip for writing an article that will go viral is to collect information from top actors or other public figures within an area (through interviews or a survey), and compile the results into an article.

3. Public Speaking

Another way to attract new customers, meet potential prospects, connect with potential partners, and become known as an expert in your industry is to engage in public speaking. If you feel like standing up in front of others and speaking is not even remotely a possibility for you, you might be missing out on some fantastic business opportunities. Most speakers are shy and feel insecure in the beginning, but it gets easier with practice and it is often well worth the effort.

How can you get more comfortable with public speaking?

Fear of public speaking is incredibly common amongst professionals at every level in the business world. For that reason, there are a multitude of tools that you can use to help overcome your fear and polish your speaking skills. One of the most popular and readily available resources is your local Toastmasters-group. Toastmasters groups are free organizations where you can gain skills and practice speaking in front of group audiences.

Another option is to have a friend record you speaking and play it back so you both can critique your speaking skills. You can also start your speaking career in less intimidating circumstances, by participating in a panel discussion for example, where not all attention is focused on you. Or you may start out by speaking at your local parent-teacher organization and other less formal, more intimate gatherings. Once you feel comfortable standing in front of people and speaking, I highly recommend submitting a proposal to a local or national translation conference or to the local chamber of commerce.

Some things to think about before creating your first public speaking engagement:

- Begin by figuring out what market you want to reach. Do you want to reach potential local clients, or establish your expertise among colleagues or clients?
- Determine where your ideal audience can be found. You might find them at the local chamber of commerce, a local translation association, or perhaps a national conference in your industry.
- Figure out what subject matter will both be relevant to your target customers and serve your business at the same time. Are you helping local businesses reach an international market? Create a speech around that topic!
- Promote the event with email marketing, blog posts and in social media to let the local

community and your target audience know about the event well in advance of the date.

- Gather information about the event and about the attendees. If possible, have the attendees sign up with their name and email, or have them leave their business card at the event. By collecting their contact information, you'll be able to follow up with potential clients and offer them your translation services.

- Give away some freebie information in the form of takeaways. You want your audience to leave feeling like they got great value out of your speech, so you may consider preparing handouts, checklists, or brochures about your services or speech topic. In whatever format you choose, your goal should be to offer excellent value to your target audience, so that hopefully they'll come back to you in the future.

- Follow up with the attendees who have indicated an interest in learning more or receiving further communication.

- Keep it up! The more you speak in public, the more confident you will become. Public speaking may become one of your more successful methods of getting new business.

 **Resources:**

Little book of PR for translators, by Nicole Y. Adams.

Master the Art of Public Speaking: How to Give a Great Speech with Confidence and Actually Enjoy Speaking in Public, by K. C. McAllister.

Further actions

Media Kit

In order to prepare for managing public relations in your translation business, I also recommend that you create a small media kit. This kit should contain information about you, your brand, and your services in one concise package. It will serve as your primary resource to equip media companies with all the pertinent information they will need to properly promote your business.

Your media kit should contain a short biography about you and your business, with information on your background, education, awards and achievements. It should also contain several high-resolution images of yourself and your company logo, in addition to any other relevant products such as books or articles you have published.

Media professionals are generally interested in stories and sources for features, such as tips on cultural differences or stories on your expertise, such as medical translation business. To pitch your PR campaign to the press you can start by creating a list of contacts at your preferred media outlets. Find out the editor's name and include a personal note with your pitch.

You can also join online communities for small business owners, which offer their members opportunities to be featured. Such promotion offers a great opportunity for exposure among professionals in other industries.

Other indirect PR and marketing tools:

- **Signature line**
  These details are often overlooked by freelance translators, but I have found that they contribute to the overall presentation of your company. Take a few moments to fully utilize the signature line in your email and customize it to include the most important information about you and your company – at the same,

time being careful not to have too much clutter. I recommend including your full name, contact information, website, language combination, and specialization.

- **Professional profile pictures**

  People prefer to buy from people they feel they know, and nothing makes people remember you as well as a picture of you. Invest in a professional profile picture to use in your online profiles, on your website, in your marketing materials and so on.

- **Letter templates and scripts**

  Letter templates and scripts are tools to help market your services and utilize your time in the most efficient way possible, i.e. save time when communicating with potential clients. I have a general letter template with information on my translation services that I use as a baseline when responding to inquiries and sending emails or letters to potential clients. I adapt the letter to fit the person I am contacting and the service or specialization in question.

I have also created email templates to respond to inquiries, for turning down jobs due to time constraints, or for contacting new potential customers. Another important script is your away message for when you are on vacation or out of the office. In the case that you will be unable to respond to an email within 24 hours, it is a good idea to turn on an auto responder explaining why you are out of the office, and when you will be back.

Because I have found that I often send similar emails over and over again, these scripts and templates have saved me enormous amounts of time typing out the same messages multiple times a week. Thanks to streamlining, I have been able to focus more of my time on the business tasks that most need my attention.

Recipe 17: *Advertising*

Another way to create awareness of your services is to use old fashion paid advertising. Not many freelance translators use paid advertising because of the costs involved to launch a paid campaign. However, others find that they can get some great returns with even a modest advertising budget. You may decide to advertise your services in print publications such as industry magazines or translation journals. Or, you may decide to apply your advertising budget to online marketing and place ads on industry websites, Google searches, or on Facebook.

I am not going to go into much detail about paid advertising, since it is the least popular method for freelance translators. However, I do hope to give you a helpful overview of the options available so that you can decide which channels to further investigate for your business.

211

- Money
- Advertising text or message

1. Print advertising

If you're interested in placing a print ad in a magazine, go to the magazine's website or read the information about publishing on the inside cover of the magazine. Journals and magazines that may be of interest for translators to advertise in are industry journals in the area of specialization, translation journals and journals or magazines issued by local chambers of commerce. However, more and more advertisers are turning to online advertising for online journals and databases and this might be more fruitful for translators, too.

2. Google AdWords

Google AdWords is used to advertise on Google and show up as a paid search result on the first page or in the side bar. You can be seen by potential customers when they are searching on Google for the things you offer. You only pay when a prospect clicks on the ad to visit your website or other site you lead them to. You can find more information about Google AdWords here:

http://en.wikipedia.org/wiki/AdWords.

3. Facebook ads

If your target clients are frequent Facebook users, you might decide that a Facebook advertising campaign is worth your investment. Facebook Ads are structured in a very similar way to Google AdWords. You pay to show up in a target audience's newsfeed or on the sidebar of their Facebook page. You can read more about Facebook Ads here:

https://www.facebook.com/business/products/ads.

Chapter 6
Entrées

After putting all the key marketing pieces in place, it's time to start using them to find and attract your prospects and ideal clients. Freelance translators at every stage in their business can struggle with the question of where to find clients and how to win both their business and their loyalty. In this chapter we'll tackle the answers to these important questions. Following these recipes will equip you with the ability to cook up your business' main course: clientele.

Where to find clients

When it comes to connecting with clients, the wonderful news for freelance translators is that potential clients are practically everywhere. They are at companies large and small, institutions in every industry, universities around the world, and there are individuals working independently. It is simply a question of getting in front of them to be able to offer your translation services.

The easiest way to gain new business is to contact translation agencies and register yourself in their ample databases. In my experience most translators are able to construct very successful careers by following this strategy. You can also find translation buyers directly, forgoing agencies altogether. For a freelance translator it is a bit harder to get in front of direct clients (the people ordering the translation), but it is by no means impossible. I know many translators that work solely with direct clients these days. It just requires a much more active marketing campaign, but can be very rewarding, since you get a personal relationship with the client. If you are the kind of person who enjoys one-on-one interaction with clients to fine-tune projects and discuss options, forging out on your own might be the right option for you. But if managing your marketing campaign independently sounds like far too much pressure, keep in mind that you can also construct a combination of agency and privately based clients.

Whether you decide to include yourself in an agency's database, or strike out on your own, there are a few ingredients you'll need to gather in order to find the clients you're looking for.

Resources for finding clients:

- Online portals and directories
- Associations of translation companies
- Industry journals
- Google search
  You can search for keyword based on your specialization, language pair and location.
- Social media platforms
  Try to find the social media platform that your ideal clients use. You can search for clients on these platforms, but more importantly follow and connect with potential clients to network with them.
- Events
  Translation conferences are great for meeting representatives from agencies, and if you are looking for direct clients, you can go to the industry conferences that they frequent. My experience is that most clients come from networking, and conferences and expos are great places to do this.
- Referrals
  If you already have clients you can use them as referrals. Every once in a while, you can ask or remind a happy client to give out your information to other people that might need translation services.

- Asking other translators for recommendations

Recipe 18: *Translation Portals and Directories*

When it comes to marketing your translation services, you'll quickly discover that not all marketing channels are created equal. Translation portals are probably the easiest way to market your services. All you have to do is sign up, fill out a profile, and then inform yourself about all the available jobs.

Unfortunately the competition for these jobs tends to be pretty steep, which affects the price pressure. However, it's also possible that clients will find you in the database and contact you directly, in which case there's no need to play the "how low can you go" price game. When filling out your profile and communicating with clients, provide as much information about your translation experience as possible. Be sure to include all the necessary profile ingredients to make your effort a success:

- Language combination
- Specialization
- Past translation/ work experience
- Education and credentials
- Memberships to translation organizations/ professional groups
- Updated resume
- Current contact information
- Portfolio with samples of your translation work, additional skills, CAT tool proficiency etc.

Registering

Most portals are pretty foolproof. They will take you through a form or a step-by-step procedure to complete your profile. In each step, try to be as specific and thorough as possible, keeping in mind that most potential clients will make judgments about your credibility and expertise based on your profile alone. This is your one chance to make a compelling first impression.

While translation portals and directories can be a powerful channel for sourcing new clients, they also come with a series of benefits and drawbacks that you should keep in mind before diving in.

Benefits:

- A quick and easy way to position your services in the industry
- Websites can be used as landing pages to provide specialized information

Drawbacks:

- Tough competition with many other translators
- Price competition can be steep
- Requires a membership
- Not a very proactive marketing method

Resources

ProZ.com has a good checklist for profile completion that you can access here:
Profiles on ProZ.com
Profiles on Translatorscafe.com

Profiles in directories such as ATA, ITI, IAPTI and more local associations

Further actions

Check out some of your colleagues' profiles on these portals and particularly those within your association's directories. Select which portal you want to register with, pay any applicable membership fees, and register your personal profile. Make it as complete (and competitive) as possible.

Recipe 19: *Translation Agencies*

In the search to find a steady stream of clients, sometimes working with a translation agency can be your best bet, without ever having to hit the streets and actively market your individual services. Once you have established yourself with a few agencies that need your language combination and specialization, chances are that clients will begin funneling into your business.

Tens of thousands of agencies all over the world are looking for freelance translators just like you, but not all agencies are created equal. In fact, experience has taught me that agencies generally come in one of three varieties: smooth-operating professional agencies, price hagglers, and shady dealers. The first (and most recommendable) category consists of highly professional and successful organizations that truly value their translators and view them as business partners. The second category consists of agencies that are purely profit-driven, and will hire and fire translators every time the wind shifts. These agencies tend to view freelance translators as commodities rather than team members, and will try to haggle and drop prices whenever possible. The third and final category is the shady dealers. These agencies have suspicious backgrounds, poor business skills, unethical practices and are likely never to complete payment for your services.

I recommend thinking of your agency as your business partner, and before you climb into bed with any agency, you'll want to interview them thoroughly and conduct your own outside research. Choosing the wrong agency can derail your translation business, while choosing the right one can reward you with a steady stream of high quality clients and a sustainable income you can be proud of.

Always research an agency before accepting work from them, and never be afraid to dump an agency if you find out that their working style is not in alignment with your values. Simply bow out as professionally as possible and keep looking for partners who will respect you and the work that you can contribute.

Ingredients

- Updated resume
- Directory or list of agencies
- Google
- PaymentPractices and/or Blue Board
- Cover letter
- Excel spreadsheet to track the following:
  - Agency names, brief description, contact information
  - When and how you first contacted them
  - Necessary follow-up steps
  - End result

1. Find agencies

You can find lists of agencies in translation association directories, translation portals, databases for payment practices, and by conducting a simple online search. No matter which method you use, make sure you research each agency before you make the first contact. Google the agency's name to see if there is a website with contact information, check ratings via PaymentPractices and/or Blueboard, ask colleagues if they have heard about the agency and so forth.

After checking credibility, you should also check whether the agency works with your particular language pair and areas of specialization. At this stage, I recommend creating a master Excel spreadsheet (as I mentioned in the ingredient list) with the agency name and a brief description about what makes that agency unique. This can help you streamline the process of contacting each one and tracking the results.

2. Contact agencies

Each agency will also have a different preferred method of communication. Some will ask you to fill out a form on their website, while others will invite you to email in your resume.

If you are asked to contact the agency by email, you can create an email template with the following information:

- **Subject line**: Include your language combination and that you are a freelance translator looking for work/clients.
- **Email body**: State that you would like to work for them as a freelance translator, highlight your accomplishments, experience, degrees and your field of specialization. Try to keep it brief, only two paragraphs.
- **Conclusion and Signature**: List your website if you have one and your contact information and ask them to check it out or contact you for further information.

3. Keep track and follow up

In your master Excel agency list, track the agencies you have contacted and follow up with an email in a week or so if you have not heard back. You can ask if they have received your email and if they have any questions or need further information.

I strongly advise against using purchased lists of agencies and spamming them with mass email campaigns containing your resume. Your goal is not to blanket the town with your resume. Your goal is to professionally and strategically target the agencies that you believe would be most interested in working with you. (Not to mention that these mass emails are impersonal and will usually never get opened.)

Benefits:

- When you are accepted into an agency, they will often provide you with a steady stream of clients

Drawbacks:

- You will earn lower rates than working directly with the clients
- Variable payment terms and methods
- May require a test translation
- Non-disclosure agreements and contracts may be required

Resources

The Insider Guide to the Strategic Marketing of Translation Services, by A.M. Sall.

Email Marketing for Translators, blog post by Jill Sommer (www.translatormusings.com).

Further actions

Take a few hours to research potential agencies. Try to get a list of 100 agencies that pass the criteria mentioned above. Contact them by their preferred method of contact. You can perhaps contact five a day, or five a week, depending on your schedule, and don't forget to follow up if you do not hear from them.

Recipe 20: *Direct Clients*

Of the marketing channels we have discussed thus far in Chapter 3, most experienced freelance translators agree that the most rewarding channel is marketing directly to the clients themselves. That means forgoing the portal pages, and skipping right over the agencies entirely. If that sounds like a risky road, it is. But it is can also be one of the most rewarding channels for your business and for you as a translator.

Direct clients are the people who will buy, publish, and use your translations – they are your final consumer. But to market directly to them and convince them that you are worthy of their business is going to require a little something extra on your end. It is going to require a very different mindset. No longer are you simply just the translator at the desk – now you are the consultant as well. This means that your job is to relate to the client, educate them, market your services and close the deal. Yes, it's a lot of work, but the end result can be a very rewarding and personal client relationship.

Luke Spear explains in his book "The Translation Sales Handbook" that: "Direct clients will not pay you more than the benefit they receive. If we understand the value our clients get from our translation, then we can optimize our pricing and offer accordingly."

Remember that you solve problems for the clients on a project basis and the client is willing to pay more to be able to use your expertise. A freelance translator who positions him- or herself as an expert or consultant will work with the client long term. The translator is not just working with a client to translate a website or marketing packet, but is solving a business language problem, or helping communicate with a new market in order to increase profits. See the difference? As a freelance translator, you are not simply providing a client with a piece of paper in a new language. You are providing a solution to a problem that previously limited their business.

Thinking of your value proposition and your business in this way is critical to being able to market directly to clients. But you are also going to have to gather a handful of other ingredients along the way:

Ingredients

- Online research
- Subscriptions to trade journals and publications
- Complete LinkedIn profile and active account
- A profile page to send out. (Not a resume, but a selling profile.)
- Brochure (optional)
- Business cards
- Resources and time to attend industry conferences, networking meetings, join trade groups, and so on.
- Database for following up and keeping track of clients
- Standard contract with your terms and conditions to protect yourself and look professional once a new direct client hires you

If you're going to start marketing directly to individuals, your first step will be to narrow down your target audience so you can focus your communication efforts. I recommend that you start with researching potential clients online in your area of expertise. Subscribe to trade journals in this area and look for industry conferences that your potential clients might attend. As much as you may not like to hear it, the truth is that most direct clients are found through networking. Therefore, you have to be prepared to devote time and resources to put yourself in front of your prospective clients.

Gather background information about your prospective clients to understand their market situation. Focus on language issues to anticipate what their needs might be and be ready to explain how you can be of service to their business. You may mention that you could reduce their lost foreign sales, time and cost of recruiting professional translators, all the while guaranteeing quality and consistency.

If these steps sound overwhelming to you, it's probably because you haven't properly narrowed down your target audience. Take some time to get clear about who your ideal clients are and where you can find them. Narrowing down to one slice of the pie

– rather than going after the entire world population – will do wonders to reduce your overwhelm. A narrow target segment will make your communication much more effective and will help you better understand what your clients need every step of the way.

1. <u>How to find direct clients</u>

- Decide on a niche and the type of companies in a specific industry that you want to target. Be specific, include size, location, type of company, etc. (I recommend writing this down so that you can always use it for future reference.)
- Identify where these companies "hang out" online and in your community. Understand how you can make contact with them. This can be through LinkedIn, a local chamber of commerce, international industry events, and so on.
- Check if you already have contacts in the industry that you can use to get in touch with your target clients.
- Look for industry-specific events in your niche that you can attend.

- Subscribe to relevant trade journals in the niche or target area and become a member in a relevant trade association.

2. Marketing to direct clients through email/mail

Sending off an email to a direct client is the easiest method of contact, but it also has a lower chance of producing positive results when compared to face-to-face networking. However, if you do decide to reach out to a potential client through their inbox, be sure that the email you send is as polished and professional as possible. The letter should have a compelling headline, define their problem and offer your solution. Show how they can benefit from using you and give a call to action. This call to action is your nudge for them to take the next step, and if they don't, simply send them a follow-up email.

Tips for contacting prospective clients by email

- Have a good headline
- Always address the person by name
- Make it relevant, short but specific
- Define their problem and offer your solution, and benefits of using your services

- Attach a PDF with your company profile
- Include a call to action
- Follow up and integrate feedback

Tips for your first attempts at contacting direct clients

- Start small
- Start with projects you truly enjoy and are very proficient in
- Look locally. It is easier to find a network locally with your potential clients, try to find someone who can give you an introduction
- Always act professionally
- Ask for feedback on every translation
- Always follow up

3. Marketing to direct clients online

- Your website is your hub for all online and offline marketing to direct clients.
- Provide useful information. Do not compare your services and skills to competitors, but do connect your solution to their problems.
- Offer more than just translation. Remember that you also have cultural knowledge.

- Give them an easy way to test your service, ex. low cost trial or free consultation.

4. Marketing to direct clients in person

Though it may not always be possible, the best way to reach potential direct clients is to meet them in person. Find industry events to attend, go to your local chamber of commerce, and make an appearance at local networking events. For more information on networking, see recipe 14.

Approach every networking opportunity with the intention of finding out more about your potential clients, ask questions about their business and markets, ask about their translation needs or problems, for example. If you strike up a good connection, you can briefly explain what you do and offer your business card or brochure in case he or she would be interested in your translation services sometime in the future. Then, always follow up after the meeting.

Unlike email communication, meeting clients in person requires a bit more advanced preparation. Here are some preparation steps to increase the chances that your next networking event is a success:

- Dress professionally and according to the dress code of the event.
- Plan ahead of time and think carefully about what you hope to achieve at each event.
- If possible, find out who will attend the event in advance. Then make a note of who you would like to get in touch with and subtly seek them out.
- Focus on a few quality contacts instead of trying to talk to as many as possible.
- Focus on creating contacts, not on making a sale.
- Arrive early or on time to evaluate the event space and get comfortable in the environment.
- If food is being served, eat first and network later.
- After the event finishes, evaluate how you did. Did you achieve your primary objective? What is one thing that you can do to improve on your networking skills before your next event?
- Follow up with all new contacts within a week after the event.

Resources:

The Translator's Sales Handbook, by Luke Spear

The Entrepreneurial Linguist, by Judy and Dagmar Jenner.
How to Succeed as a Freelance Translator, by Corinne McKay.

Further actions

Marketing to direct clients is a continuous project that takes time. Be patient and kind with yourself, and don't expect miraculous results over night.

Remember, you are transitioning from freelancer to consultant, and the most important ingredient for success is your mindset. Read the books that I recommend in the References section to create a marketing plan that will get in front of your ideal direct clients and market your services to them.

Once again, if you find that you are lost in overwhelm or don't know where to begin, always work on narrowing down your target audience. Narrow it down to a very specific niche and/or location and start from there. Then leverage the resources in your area, tap into your personal network, and never underestimate the value of your existing contacts and LinkedIn.

Chapter 7
Side Dishes

There is no other issue discussed more frequently in the freelance translation world than pricing, and yet somehow revealing your rate to other translators is taboo.

As a beginning translator, determining what to charge (and sticking to it) is often the biggest hurdle to overcome in establishing your business in the translation industry. For more experienced translators there are other issues concerning pricing to wonder about. Numerous questions arise, such as: should I charge per word, per hour or per project? How can I raise my prices?

These pricing struggles are all challenges that I have lived firsthand in starting and running my own translation business. I know the discomfort, the uncertainty, and the frustration that they present. But I also know that they can be solved with a little strategic thinking and determination. In this chapter I will walk you through all of these questions and help you clarify the right answers to the pricing doubts that you may be facing in your own business.

Why am I talking about pricing strategies in a marketing book? Because your prices and pricing strategies indirectly affect your marketing strategies. In fact, pricing strategies are so important for your freelance business success, that I have devoted a separate chapter for it.

Recipe 21: *Pricing strategies for your translation services*

Once you have a solid business foundation, with all the skills and knowledge you need to create high quality translations and a steady stream of clients knocking on your door, you're going to have to answer one all-important question: What do I charge?

Before explaining how to determine your rate, I would like to bring up the different options for pricing. Translators often quote their rates on a per-unit basis. The unit can be per word, per character, per line, or per page, and the per-unit rate is usually based on the source text.

However, sometimes unit-based pricing is not ideal for your translation projects because the units you produce don't always look the same, or do not take the same amount of time to produce. The main advantage with per unit pricing is that everyone knows up front how much the translation will cost. Having a per-unit rate allows the client to anticipate exactly what your final invoice will be, which ultimately makes it easier for him or her to buy from you.

But is it in your best interest to establish a per-unit rate? Well, yes and no. If you can be efficient when translating, you can usually earn more if you charge by unit than what the client would be willing to pay for an hourly rate (the second pricing structure). The main advantage of pricing by the hour is that there is no risk of loss for the translator, plus it is a common unit in other businesses, and easy to understand for clients not used to the business of translation and counting units.

The last option I want to bring up is to charge per project. This usually works best with direct clients, where you can take into account time for research, formatting, and editing. Direct clients may also prefer to be quoted a total price. So let's take a look at how you can determine your price:

Ingredients

- Your cost of living
- Your target annual income
- How much you can work
- How much the client is willing to pay
- Industry rates
- Rate calculation tools
- Language combination, and estimated demand
- Your location

Steps

1. Determine what your monthly costs are and how much you need to earn in order to break even. (These calculations can be done on a per-year basis, just make sure that all your numbers have the same units.)

2. Take the amount from Step 1 and add the amount of extra money you would like to earn per month.

3. Establish how much you can (or want to) work per month/year. Then break it down into days and hours to arrive at an hourly income.

4. Establish how much you need to translate per hour or day to meet your

goal. The best way to do this is to keep records of how much you translate, for how long, and how much you earn over a certain period of time. This will give you the best indicator of how much you need to translate.

5. Compare your target rate to industry standards, based on your language combination and specialization. You can do this by looking at rate surveys or asking around among colleagues and potential clients.

6. Take into account non-billable time, such as time for invoicing, project administration, research and marketing.

7. Set your per-word/character/page/hour rate based on this estimation.

8. Adjust as necessary. Do not base your rate on a fear of charging too much. Instead base the rate on how much you want to work, who you want to work for and of course a balance of supply and demand.

Resources

ProZ.com's rate calculator (www.proz.com/translator-rates-calculator/).

CAL Pro – rate calculator for translators (http://www.atanet.org/business_practices/calpro_us.php).

UK version of Cal Pro (http://www.ecpdwebinars.co.uk/sitefiles/19/7/5/197552/CalPro_v1_3_EN-GB.xls).

Jonathan Hine's pamphlet "I am worth it! How to set your price, and other tips for freelancers," available from http://www.scriptorservices.com/buybook/.

Local translation associations also perform rate surveys from time to time. Please contact your local association to see if they have one, or ask your colleagues. I am aware of surveys from American Translators Association and BDU (German translators association), but I am sure there are more.

Further actions

Once you have determined your rate, you can divide it into a minimum rate. This minimum rate represents your price floor, which you do not drop below. Then estimate an ideal rate, which is your "sweet spot" and the amount that you would like to work in order to maintain your desired lifestyle.

Once these two bars are set, do not ever go below your minimum rate. Sometimes clients can come back to you after receiving a quote and ask for a slight reduction. The best thing to do is to be firm and not accept. Try to prove why you are worth what you are asking for and be willing to be turned down. Don't see this as a defeat, but instead as a chance to find a better paying client.

Recipe 22: *Pricing Structure*

Aside from your per unit rate, you also need to consider other pricing factors such as discounts, rush charges and other related charges. Taking these additional variables into account will allow you to construct a pricing structure that will guide you through the majority of situations your business will encounter over the years.

Some freelance translators skip these steps, and opt to evaluate each individual project as it arises. However, this can quickly become a phenomenal headache and consumes much more time than simply adhering to a single standard pricing structure. Though you may have to invest several hours in order to determine all the discounts and fees that you will build into your business, my experience has taught me that it is well worth the initial effort.

Ingredients

- Volume discounts
- CAT tool-based discounts for repetitions and fuzzy matches
- Rush charges
- Weekend work
- Charges related to source formatting, Desktop Publishing
- Your minimum fee

Steps

1. **Volume discounts**

   Many agency clients ask for discounts if they can provide large volumes of work. In general, volume discounts do not make much sense for translators. Agencies often have the misconception that translators will be able to turn out projects significantly faster after they become familiar with the first few projects. While this may be true to some small degree, turnaround times tend to stay fairly consistent and certainly don't decrease enough to justify price discount. In my experience, translators that offer a volume discount end up working for less for the same amount of time. Consider the project carefully before accepting a volume discount, or decide to not accept volume discounts at all.

2. **CAT tool-based discounts**

   Another common discount request from agencies is a discount for repetitions and fuzzy matches. These discounts are only in your best interest if the TM is very good, if you are very familiar with the project and know that high matches in the source text will lead to high matches in the target text too, and that the surrounding sentences will not need to be modified as well.

   Think carefully about whether you want to accept these discounts as it can mean a significant reduction in your income and negate the benefit of investing in a CAT tool in the first place. The only way these types of discounts make sense is if working with the CAT tool significantly increases your productivity. If you can process more volume by using the tool, then you can think about offering some discount. However, always ensure that the amount of discount is proportional to your productivity gains.

3. **Rush charges**

   Some translators charge a rush charge for expedited turnaround times, and some don't. If you decide to charge a rush charge, you will first need to determine what exactly constitutes a rush project.

   Is it a certain number of words within a certain time period, or is it when you have to work evenings or nights and rearrange your schedule to fit the job in? You also need to determine how much your rush charge should be. Is it 10%, 50% or 100% extra? It is important to set clear limits and be honest with the client. When to charge a rush charge can also be a personal decision. For example, I usually do not charge extra for a few hundred words by the end of the day, but if a client needs more than 3000 words before the next day, I charge a rush fee if I can take the project on.

Deciding to incorporate a rush charge into your pricing structure can also help to ensure that the job is really worth your while. If you are going to lose sleep in order to complete a client's project on time, make sure that your earnings justify the elevated stress; otherwise you are likely to be frustrated and turn in a sub-par quality – meaning that nobody wins in the end.

4. **Weekend work**

    You have to determine whether you will accept weekend work or not and whether you will charge extra for it. Many translators accept weekend work and charge extra for it, because these projects may cause them to miss weekend plans and arrange for additional babysitting.

    Some translators view their service as 7 days a week and do not change their rates for this type of work. I try to avoid working weekends. If I do work weekends it might be because I was tied up with non-work related tasks during work hours, and then I do not charge extra for it. However, if I receive a project at 5 pm on a Friday night, with a deadline of Monday morning, I do charge extra if I decide to take it on for some reason.

5. **Extra charges for formatting**

    It is perfectly normal to charge extra if you have to do formatting work on top of your translation work. For example if you receive a PDF file you may need to process with an OCR tool and format the target file before delivering the final project. Documents scanned as images and faxed documents produce other formatting issues to take into consideration. The most common way to charge for these is an extra hourly rate.

6. **Minimum fees**

    You should also determine a minimum fee for each project. This can be a charge for one hour for small jobs, or slightly below that.

    Why should freelance translators charge minimum fees? Because even if the translation only has 50 words, you still need to check the context and references, you still need to proofread and spell check and you still need to do all the administrative work around the project, such as apply a translation memory if one exists, invoice and deliver – all of which takes extra time. A minimum fee for translation work is thus very reasonable, even though the amount of work might seem very small.

Resources

ProZ.com Wiki: Determining your rates as a freelance translator. What is "the right rate" for your translation services? by Corinne McKay (www.thoughtsontranslation.com).

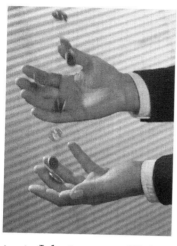

In every industry and at every pay grade, asking for a raise can feel a little bit like navigating through a mine field – you know you want to get to the other side, but taking the steps to get there can be quite nerve-wracking. However, if you do so with confidence and tact, I bet you will be pleasantly surprised by what you can accomplish.

My rule of thumb is that if you are working with direct clients you can usually ask for a raise every year, adjusting to inflation, or simply quote higher for any new projects that arise. Negotiating a raise with an existing translation agency and their clients is a whole different story. In fact, many of them simply aren't open to having the conversation at all.

If you do believe that you deserve a raise (or feel the need to raise your rates), simply follow this recipe and leave the stress out of the mix.

- Negotiation skills
- Facts to back up and motivate your increase
- Steady work
- New clients
-

1. Know the optimum moments to ask for a raise or to set your rates higher:
   a. When you are taking on new clients
   b. When you are already very busy and get a new inquiry
   c. At the beginning of a new year (make sure that you warn clients in advance that your rates will increase after a specific date).

2. You can bring up your rates to your current level with agencies you have not worked with for a long time and who are now contacting you with a new project. However, you may risk losing the new project.

3. You can try to induce minimal, continuous increases to existing clients, adjusting to inflation. This is not as painful for clients as a substantial increase.

4. Asking for more money is a negotiation. Hone your negotiation skills and realize you might lose.

5. Make sure you justify the price increase and be able to explain your reasoning if a client asks about the change. You may explain that you've acquired new translation tools, taken a course to continue your education, or you have new and improved expertise.

6. Raise previous clients' rates to be on par with those of newer clients. You can justify a rate increase by saying something like, "I really enjoy working with you, but most of my other clients are paying me XX. In order for me to be able to continue being available for you and prioritizing you as a client, I would like to ask if you can meet my current rate."

7. You can raise your rates by finding new clients in higher-paying countries.

8. There is usually a ceiling for how much or how often you can raise your rates with agencies. Once you have reached this ceiling you have to move over to direct clients if you want to earn more.

9. By being confident and clear about your raise and when it will take effect, you come off as professional and easy to work with. After all,

no one wants to receive a surprisingly large invoice out of the blue, so be as transparent as you can.

10. You can start earning more by dropping some of your lowest paying clients so you have more time to focus on existing or new, better-paying clients.

Resources

Raising your translation rates: how and when, by Corinne McKay (www.throughsontranslation.com).

How to raise your freelance pay rates in the next 60 days, by Carol Tice (www.makealivingwriting.com)

Further actions

As with any salary negotiation, you need to do some preparation beforehand. Before raising a rate or renegotiating a price, make sure you have your arguments clear and have polished your negotiation skills. Approach the conversation with confidence and a cool head, and be able to accept that you may lose some clients, but that you may also make room in your schedule for clients of even higher caliber. Good luck!

Chapter 8
Desserts

You've almost made it to the end of the cookbook! You have stocked your pantry with the right training and specialties, filled the table with delicious appetizers and a firm marketing foundation, satiated yourself with an entrée of client-sourcing strategies, crafted side dishes and price structures, and now I hope you have a little appetite left over for dessert.

These are the elements that round out your meal and end it on high note. As you may know, not everyone is a dessert person; some prefer to leave the table before the sweet treats are brought out. That's perfectly fine. Here are some things that are not necessarily part of your marketing arsenal, but nonetheless are wonderful tools and tips that will make your work as a freelance translator more fulfilling and complete.

Your long-term success as a freelance translator depends on how well you can keep your existing customers, and continually earn their repeat business. When you successfully transform a one-time customer into repeat business, that is when you gain customer loyalty. But why is customer loyalty so important? Well, for one thing is a lot cheaper to keep current clients happy than it is to find new ones.

Imagine all the time and effort that goes into finding a potential client lead, pitching your services, negotiating a contract, securing and completing the first job. All for just one single client! If you had to repeat that lengthy process for every translation project, you would likely die of exhaustion – or at the very least, exhaust all your valuable resources. As a savvy business owner, you want to keep that same customer – who is already in your network – coming back for more and more projects, which means you won't have to go fishing for new clients nearly as frequently.

I recommend creating relationships or partnerships with your clients to keep you on the top of their minds. This means that you stay visible and present so that the next time a translation project surfaces, you are the first person your clients think to turn to. It is not enough to simply provide good quality translations – that is what is expected of you, and it is exactly what all your competition is up to. You have to not only provide good quality translations, but an outstanding customer service experience as well. Here is how to do it:

Ingredients

- Partnership
- Communication
- Service
- Reliability
- Respect
- Confidentiality
-

Steps

1. Provide the best possible quality. This means understanding what your clients' expectations are and living up to them to the best of your ability. The more you understand what your

clients need, the more you will be able to deliver.

2. Always, always meet deadlines. Do everything in your power to keep deadlines. Evaluate the project before accepting to make sure the deadline is reasonable for you. If despite your best efforts you cannot keep the deadline, you must deal with the situation immediately and professionally. Offer solutions to the client and maintain open communication at all times.

3. Follow instructions, even if you think that some steps are unnecessary. Check before delivering that you have followed the instructions. This sometimes requires that you deliver a project before deadline, giving the client ample time to review your work and make changes as necessary.

4. Be available more often than not and be easy to contact.

5. Confirm receipt of all communication.

6. Provide referrals if you are not available. The client will remember your service and as long

as you provide good quality translations, the client will not stop using your services in favor of the referral. Let your clients know in advance of your holidays and when you will not be available, and help them find someone else during that time.

7. Keep yourself informed of the client's business and make sure you know what their problems and needs are.

8. Show appreciation to your clients. Send thank you notes and holiday cards, thank them for their payment.

9. Keep in touch with the client regularly. Provide updates about your services and availability, new skills and tools etc., or send them an email when you notice something new with their company.

10. Honor the client's confidentiality.

Further actions

View your relationship with each customer as a partnership. Your success should contribute to your customer's success and vice versa. This starts with open and direct communication. Clarify mutual expectations, which can vary for each customer or project contact.

Remember that you work in the service sector and deal with real people. Be courteous, helpful and reliable to make sure the project manager will choose you out of the other translators in the database.

I find that it is always helpful to remember that your clients have selected you out of all the other options available to them. No matter what language combination or specialty you are working with, there is always competition. Your quality customer service, transparent and frequent communication, and the small ways you go beyond their expectations are the ways you stand out to your clients. More importantly, these are the practices that make you worthy of their repeat business.

For most freelance translators the ebb and flow of projects is one of the most frustrating aspects of the freelance lifestyle. One week you are working 12-hour days and have more work than you can handle, while another the inbox is bone dry and you do not know when the next project will come in. This is called the feast and famine cycle.

Some freelancers simply accept this whirlwind cycle as an unavoidable fact of life, something we simply have to put up with and adjust to. I disagree – to some degree. I believe that there are some very proactive measures every freelancer can take in order to avoid falling victim to this vicious cycle. In this section, we're going to explore ways that you can take back the reigns of your freelance business.

Ingredients

- Marketing
- Customer care and contact
- Time management and project scheduling
- Savings
- Budgeting
- Business development

Steps

1. **Market continually**

   One of the most important things to do in order to avoid the vicious famine cycle is to market a little bit continually. It is easy to forget your marketing efforts when you are busy with work, but if we wait until the work dries up, it will only take longer to recover from the famine. I recommend setting aside time every day (or every week) to do take some focused marketing actions. Whether its 1 hour a day or 3 hours a week, this time should be used to fine tune your marketing strategy and actively connect with new client leads.

2. **Build a buffer in savings**

   Nothing will ease your fears and doubts like a monetary safety net. Having a little extra savings set aside will help you stay focused when you hit a famine cycle and it will keep you from accepting work that is not right for you. Save a little bit every month so that you end up with about 3 months of savings that cover the living expenses - not your income - just your expenses.

3. **Create a budget**

   Pick one of your lowest month's income levels from the last year and use it as a baseline for budgeting your expenses. Figure out how much you need to earn to cover necessary expenses and work with that. Take seasonal variations and other factors such as vacation into consideration. At the end of the year you can reevaluate your baseline and adjust your spending and saving accordingly.

4. **Prioritize regular clients**

   Try to prioritize clients that can give you regular work to cover your bases. Build up enough regular clients and you will avoid most famine cycles altogether. Sometimes you might have to turn down new work to give your existing clients priority if they can provide more regular work. Try to develop long-term customer relationships and focus on providing good service to the clients you already have.

5. **Develop better negotiation skills**

   Sometimes a little bit of negotiation can go a long way. You can try to negotiate your projects and deadlines to avoid having too much work or too little at the same time. Direct clients can have more flexible deadlines.

6. **Improve your time management**

   If you are not using your time efficiently, it can seem like you have too much to do, or that you do not get the most important things done. Bad time management can also keep you from spending enough time on marketing. I will discuss time management in detail in the following section.

Resources

How to avoid the feast and famine cycle – by Ed Gandia

(www.freelancefolder.com).

7 easy ways to control the infamous feast or famine cycle – by Laura Spencer

(http://freelancem.ag/freelancing-basics/freelancer-feast-or-famine-cycle/).

Further actions

Sit down with your calendar right now and block out scheduled periods of time to tackle each of the six tasks mentioned in the recipe above. Perhaps schedule a 2-hour period to sit down and really craft a budget that will work for you, or 30 minutes to transfer money into savings for your 3-month safety net. Or perhaps you decide to take a course or read a book on positive time management techniques.

Dedicate this month, or the next two months, to creating your famine-feast survival guide. Having tools in place will help you better control your workload and your work-life balance. They will also help alleviate the panic that accompanies famine times. Just remember that everything is cyclical and that some things are simply beyond your control. If you are taking proactive measures to protect yourself and your business, and if you use famine times to seek clients and rejuvenate your marketing, then you will be back on track in no time.

Balance

One of the biggest challenges a freelance translator faces is learning how to efficiently and effectively manage time. If we cannot manage our time well, we end up working long hours, often inefficiently, and can easily start despising our work.

Long and irregular work hours seem to be a norm among freelancers, but it does not have to be this way. In fact, I am a living testament and firm believer that it should not be this way! Many highly successful freelance translators do not work long or irregular hours. Instead, they have learned to manage their time efficiently so that they have time for other things in life. As a result, they enjoy their work more and know the importance of having time for their families, recharging their batteries, and keeping a distance to their freelance work in order to be able to do a good job.

Most of us became freelance translators in order to enjoy the benefits of being our own bosses, to be able to somewhat control our own work flows and schedules. However, being able to do so requires that we proactively manage our time and clients, rather than being at the mercy of a hundred different demands all streaming in during a single week. Here's my recipe for creating a more manageable work-life balance:

Ingredients

- Time tracking
- To-do list
- Organization skills
- Fixed work hours
- Goals and plans
- Activities for stress release

Steps

1. **Track your time**

   In order to develop and learn time management strategies we have to know where our time is going right now. This takes time, but if you look at the way you manage your time currently you will hopefully notice patterns and things you can change or do more efficiently. Create a tracking sheet and set aside time every day for a month or so to record how you spend your time.

How often do you get interrupted? How long does it take to complete certain tasks? By tracking the time you spend each day, week and month on work activities, you will be able to calculate how much you are making per hour. This can encourage you to become more efficient with your time, instead of just working more hours.

2. **Make a list**

   At the beginning of each day, make a list with everything you need to do for that day and prioritize the tasks. Literally number each one in the order you will complete it and make a time estimate of how long you will spend on each one. This will help keep you working at a reasonable pace and ensure that your schedule isn't derailed by any one single task. Then, when you complete a task, cross it off the list and congratulate yourself on making progress.

3. **Prioritize organization**

   In order to achieve maximum efficiency with your time, you need to be organized – and stay organized throughout the week. Keep an organized office so you don't have to waste time looking for things and have as few distractions as possible. Keep your finances organized so you don't have to spend time figuring out which clients owe you money. Have an organized schedule so you don't waste time between activities.

   I recommend spending the final 15-20 minutes of every working day organizing your desk, updating client files, and making your to-do list for the upcoming workday. Clear off your desk and leave everything as neat and organized as possible. This will ensure that when you step into your office the next day, you're on a high note, rather than feeling overwhelmed from the previous day's mess.

4. **Outsource**

   Once you are earning a fairly steady income you can start focusing on tasks that you do well and try to outsource tasks that you dislike doing or that you are very inefficient at. For example, I outsource all my bookkeeping and accounting, since I am not good at it, I dislike doing it, it takes a long time, and my time is better spent translating and earning money. I am also outsourcing the house cleaning, so that I can spend the little free time I have with my family doing more fun things. You will be more efficient and hopefully earn more if you find things that you can outsource to people that do them better, faster and/or cheaper, so you can focus on what you do best and like doing the most.

5. **Set a deadline**

   Most of our projects as freelance translators already come with set deadlines. But what about marketing tasks or continuing education? Set tentative deadlines for these tasks too, otherwise they may never get done, or take longer time than they have to. My rule of thumb is that if it doesn't exist on my calendar, it doesn't exist at all. Schedule in time for all the short, medium, and long term projects that you want to complete this year.

6. **Make the most out of small pockets of time**
   Keep a list of things that you can do in less than 15 minutes and keep it close at hand. There will be opportunities every day with these pockets of time that you can fill with these tasks.

   Meetings are late, your children's practice is going over time, or you are waiting in a doctor's office. These pockets are perfect for replying to some emails, making phone calls, preparing for a meeting, confirming appointments, or mapping out a project outline. With 15 minutes of focused work, you can often get more done than in one hour of unfocused work.

7. **Focus on one task at a time**
   If you work from home, there are always plenty of things that can distract you. As much as we would love to believe otherwise, the truth is that multitasking is not at all efficient. Try to focus on one task at a time.

   Keep a notebook next to you so that when you think of things that are not related to the task at hand, you can make a short note of them and then get back to them later when you are finished with what you are working on, or perhaps save them for those 15-minute pockets of time mentioned above. Turn off email and social media so you can focus on one thing at a time. Set a timer for 25-50 minutes and only focus on your task during this time. When the timer rings, you can take a break and check email, put in a load of laundry, or something else for 10-15 minutes before you start your next focus time period.

8. **Have a set ending time**

   Whether you believe me or not, you will become more efficient if you know you have to stop working at a certain time each and every day. For freelancers, there is always the temptation to keep working late into the night in order to get things done.

   Of course late night shifts might be inevitable some of the time, but you are usually more productive if you know you have to finish by a specific time, especially if you have something fun and relaxing to look forward to afterward. Push yourself to stay on schedule and efficiently work your way through the daily to-do list. Then, when you make it to the bottom of the list, turn off your computer, step away from your cell phone and reward yourself for a hard day's work.

9. **Have goals and a plan for your time**

   If you have a goal to work toward, it is much easier to stay focused until you reach that goal. Set minor goals for your week or your day, such as accomplishing a specific task by a certain time to keep you focused and productive. The same thing goes for planning. If you have a plan for your time you are less likely to waste time. You can plan your work a week at a time, for the next day or at the beginning of each day.

10. **Keep a work-life balance and do not overwork**

    Many freelancers work long hours, mostly because they have their own company and think it is quite fun to develop their business. But we all have a need for work/life balance and working too much can have disastrous effects on your health, well-being, your family and your efficiency and productivity. With a more realistic work schedule you will be able to improve focus and have more energy for completing tasks efficiently. (Not to mention that you will be able to fully enjoy the work that you do and the business you run.)

11. Have an activity for stress release

Freelance work can be quite stressful. We have many deadlines to meet and often have to deal with difficult clients and last-minute problems. Stress can usually not be avoided but we can learn how to manage stress in a positive way. I recommend trying to find an activity that helps you relax. For some this activity is exercise-oriented for others it can involve music, art, friends, or just going for a walk. These activities should be enjoyable for you and provide perspective to your everyday work tasks.

 Resources
13 Principles of Effective Time Management for Freelancers, by Steven Snell (www.Designmag.com).

6 Practical Time Management Strategies for Freelancers and Solos, by Ed Gandia (www.internationalfreelancersacademy.com.)

Time Management Tools I like

1. RescueTime – allows you to keep track of how you spend your time on your computer and lets you analyze how this time was spent.
2. Focus Booster (for the Pomodoro technique) – an online timer with 25 minutes of work followed by 5 minutes of rest, which helps you segment tasks and get them done.
3. Toggl – a free time-tracking app to track time with a single click and easily switch between different tasks and create reports.
4. Evernote – with Evernote, you can collect and find good ideas, images or audio clips from your PC or phone and sync them for easy retrieval no matter where you are.

Further actions

It is important to achieve a good work/life balance, and chances are that the biggest obstacles to achieving this balance are thoughts swirling around in your head right at this very moment. Get out of your head, and into taking action. You have to define what works for you and what doesn't. You have to define how you want your life to be. No one else can do it for you.

There is always a belief that we should be doing this or that, work more on this project or make a certain amount of money because someone else does. Set reasonable expectations, according to your own values, and do not measure them against anyone else's.

Allow your freelance translation business to empower you to set positive, healthy boundaries and put into practice the techniques to make your time more effective.

Chapter 9
Conclusion

You might not feel like a five-star chef just yet, but I hope I have increased your appetite for marketing your translation services and creating the career and lifestyle you deserve. My goal with this book was to create an easy to follow guide that you can refer back to when developing certain marketing tactics.

By now you should have some recipes or formulas to follow that will make marketing your translation services easier. You are better equipped with tools for your business, you know some methods and systems to target and reach your ideal clients, plus have some cooking skills or strategies to grow your translation business and enjoy the process. Remember, this is a constantly evolving process.

If you think there are some recipes missing in this marketing cookbook, feel free to contact me through www.marketingtipsfortranslators.com, or let me know if you would like some personal guidance. I would love to hear from you. Good luck with cooking up the career and lifestyle you want as a freelance translator!

Appendix

Marketing Plan for Freelance Translators

About My Business
Summarize your current business situation, sales, income.

My Business Goals
Describe your goals for the next 12 months.

My Products and/or Services
What you offer, what it does for customers, why it's unique.

My Target Market
Who is your ideal customer? Where can you find them?

My Marketing Activities
What promotional methods will you focus on this year?

Others

My Marketing Calendar
Plan the promotions, sales, media, & other strategies you'll use. Consider holidays and other events in your planning.

January	February
March	April
May	June
July	August
September	October
November	December

278

Made in the USA
Lexington, KY
16 December 2014